Spring

I0169561

CONNECT

A Daily Interactive Guide to Connect Us with Being and Beauty

by

Don Carroll

Dedication

To the Volunteers and Clients of the North Carolina Lawyer Assistance Program

© 2008-2009 William Donald Carroll, Jr.
Photographic images are the property of Wayne Morris and Ann Ehringhaus.
All rights reserved.

A Navajo Prayer Song

Today I will walk out, today everything will leave me,
I will be as I was before, I will have a cool breeze over my body,
I will have a light body, I will be happy forever,
nothing will hinder me.
I walk with beauty before me. I walk with beauty behind me.
I walk with beauty below me. I walk with beauty above me.
I walk with beauty around me. My words will be beautiful.

In beauty all day long may I walk.
Through the returning seasons, may I walk.
On the rail marked with pollen may I walk.
With dew about my feet, may I walk.

With beauty before me may I walk.
With beauty behind me may I walk.
With beauty below me may I walk.
With beauty above me may I walk.
With beauty all around me may I walk.

In old age wandering on a trail of beauty,
lively, may I walk.
In old age wandering on a trail of beauty,
living again, may I walk.
My words will be beautiful.

Acknowledgement

The idea for this book initially was modest. It was to collect into one place a workbook of tools for people to use to facilitate their personal growth. All of these tools work best if they are practiced daily. Like many of you I have read a daily meditation for years. It didn't take long to realize that connecting these tools with a daily meditation was the most practical way for people to incorporate helpful new practices into their lives.

For a number of years, as director of the North Carolina Lawyer Assistance Program, I have worked with individuals suffering from addictive disease, mental illness and just plain unhappiness. The most common feature of these illnesses and the experience of normal healthy people who feel their lives are unfulfilling is a lack of connection. The focus then of each daily meditation, and the tools that go with them, is to provide a way for greater connection, with self, others, the natural world, Beauty, and meaning greater than ourselves.

Not too long into this project, I realized that providing access to greater connection via the printed word is limited by the medium itself. An image that arouses curiosity and emotional interest creates a different and potentially broader experience of connection. Through the good fortune of working with Ann Ehringhaus and Wayne Morris, two gifted photographers, it has been possible to add intriguing, striking and contemplative images to this assembly of tools and written meditations. I am deeply grateful to Ann and Wayne for the contribution of their photographic skills and for their dedication to being a part of this project.

This book would also not be possible without those who have supported me in my own spiritual growth during the past years. I am grateful to my Friends at the Davidson Friends Meeting. I have been continuously supported by my Davidson Spiritual Directors' peer group, which includes Ann Starette, Clarence Fox, Jane Pope and Linda Beauregard. I have also been fortunate to be a member of a Winston Salem Spiritual Directors' peer group and I am particularly grateful for the support from that group of Nancy Cannon, Betty Haywood, Martha Harper and Phillip Squire. In addition, I have been a part of the Davidson United Methodist Church's Spiritual Formation Program led by Ann Starrette. Ann has taught me how to carry a vision fiercely and gently at the same time. I am indebted to the Spiritual Formation peer group under Ann's care, especially John Drayer, Nicole Greer, Mary Beth Huskey, Kate Tullis and Mary Boyce. To my own Spiritual Director, Dr. Bill Pierce, a deep, deep thank you.

Creativity is an important aspect of spiritual development. I have had the opportunity to be a member of a splendid poetry writing group for the past ten years. I am particularly grateful to its members: Bob Cumming, Tootsie O'Hara, Lou Green, Gilda Syverson, Ann Campanella, Larry Sorkin and Suzanne Leitner. All of those mentioned in this acknowledgement, most without knowing it, nurtured this project.

In addition, I am deeply grateful for the efforts of Tootsie O'Hara, John Pastryk and Pam Dykstra in reading the manuscript and offering many helpful suggestions and much encouragement. Pam Dykstra did angelic double duty in final manuscript review – many, many thanks Pam.

Completing this project would have been impossible without the long-suffering help of Buffy Holt, my Administrative Assistant, who never flinched when I often needed to return the manuscript to her to implement additional editing corrections. Buffy's technical skills and writerly eye for form and presentation were immensely helpful. Buffy, I'm deeply grateful for all your help.

Introduction

We experience love, joy and equanimity through connection – through connection to our self, to a meaning greater than us, and to others. This book is designed for ordinary healthy people to use as a pilgrimage into a deeper experience of connection to their own lives. This book is a path and set of practices for connection, or deeper re-connection, with the vitality and Mystery of life. In addition, this book is designed for those, like many of us, who have struggled with addictions, depression or other mental illnesses that have kept us cut off from vibrant, vital lives.

The most salient aspect of all addictive disease, mental illness and just plain unhappiness is loss of connection. Connection to the things that ground us most in our lives – nature, people we love, creative work, creative play, creative art, a Power greater than ourselves, and the path to connect with all of these.

In our modern culture we experience intersecting currents of disconnection. First, many of the traditional paths of connection, such as those found in traditional religions, have lost their vitality. Secondly, with our many means of instant communication, or perhaps because of them, our culture is more fragmented than ever. And thirdly, life events can inevitably be experienced as disconnecting. We at some point have to get through adolescence. We lose the parents that brought us into this world. A career can go stale and change become necessary. So the process of needing to connect, or re-connect, continues throughout our lives. Sometimes, however, we let the busyness of living, what seems important but really isn't, or a disease state open the space of disconnection to an alarming gap.

Out of the modern chaos of fragmentation and disconnection, three paths to reconnect with self, meaning greater than ourselves, and others remains open. These paths are archetypal in dimension and universal in appeal. There are the paths of Beauty, Truth and Goodness. The connections that vitalize our lives occur through our heart, through our emotional nature, through the part of us that values. When these connections are fulfilling, we experience them as Beauty, Truth and Goodness.

From an Enneagram perspective an initial year of practice focusing on the meditation practices using your dominant type is most important to initially raise awareness. For the second year of meditation a practiced focus on your repressed center of your type is exceedingly helpful.

Here is a suggested approach to make these practices most vital.

First Year Path of Dominant Enneagram Center

The Way of Truth – Enneagram Types 5, 7 & 3, or 9
The Way of Beauty – Enneagram Types 2, 4 & 6 or 9
The Way of Goodness – Enneagram Types 1, 8 & 6 or 3

Second Year Path of Repressed Enneagram Center

The Way of Truth – Enneagram Types 2, 1 & 6
The Way of Beauty – Enneagram Types 7, 8 & 3
The Way of Goodness – Enneagram Types 4, 5 & 9

Which of these three paths is the most suitable for each of us depends upon our natural personality predisposition. The Enneagram divides personality types into three different groups: those who meet the world either mentally, emotionally or instinctively. Personality type thus tells us our basic approach to making meaning in the world. Knowing our dominant approach and our repressed center offers us a choice of deciding which path is most helpful to us in our personal growth:

> the way of the intellect – the way of truth
> the way of the heart – the way of beauty
> the way of the instincts or will – the way of goodness

Any experience can be viewed as a blessing or a curse. There is always a choice of perspective, but it is not always an easy choice. Sometimes, as in grief, we must be in the place of darkness for a while. This book takes the perspective that any difficult transition is always enhanced through the process of connection and that ultimately all connections express Beauty. Even in the worst, most painful experience it is possible to see benefits – growth in one's relationship with God, the development of compassion, or a deepened understanding of a certain type of human affliction. Certain difficult things in life we must all do ourselves, but none has to be done alone. This book is not about making our lives easier, or happier. Rather, it is about making the internal experience of our lives deeper, richer, a more shared experience and an experience connected to Beauty.

Connection is important because it is the way our brains have been shaped. We are unique as a species in that much of our brain development occurs after birth. This process is possible only because as infants we learned how to attach to our parents. Our brains grow up in the reality of the unconscious minds of our parents. Their ways of responding to our needs shape our personalities and perceptions of the world, and ultimately shape the architecture of our brains.

Because of this developmental process our brains are inescapably social, and drive us to connect to something outside of ourselves all of our lives. This drive to connect is survival based. It is complicated by the fact that we really have three different brains. At the core is the reptilian brain responsible for instincts – for eating, mating and surviving. It is surrounded by the limbic system that controls learning, memory and emotion. On top of this is the neo-cortex that organizes our thoughts and imagination. The challenge is that these three brains are like three different computers running on three different operating systems. With good enough parents the early brain building will serve us reasonably well in adulthood. When parental patterns of addiction and mental illness shape the baby brain, though this architecture may enhance the child's early survival, unconscious patterns are created that do not work long-term.

For example, if the child's reptilian survival brain is forced to operate as a response to abuse, with defenses of disassociation or hyper-control, and is insufficiently balanced by the later developing neo-cortex, this child may end up never able in adulthood to establish the healthy connections needed for human flourishing.

Neurobiology shows us that contemporary psychological approaches have as of now failed to live up to their promise in overcoming the difficulty of bringing the three different operating systems on line together. It is often the unconscious lack of communication between the survival, emotional and intellectual brains that manifest itself in addictive patterns, mental illness and just plain unhappiness.

While the many different versions today of Freud's "talking cure" can help ameliorate the underlying maladaptive connection patterns in the brain structure, what has been missing in the world of psychology is a way to dramatically reboot these three computers into a more synergistic harmony.

This missing possibility has always been a part of the spiritual world. This possibility can be found in diverse stories: Paul's experience on the road to Damascus; the white light experience of Bill Wilson, cofounder of AA in Townes Hospital; or in the prescription of Carl Jung to a seemingly hopeless alcoholic that his only chance to get better was a spiritual experience. The spiritual traditions tell us there is a dramatic way to change. The process of how this occurs is called Grace. Grace is non-linear. Grace does not occur by our own wills, but occurs by our internal connection to something greater than ourselves outside of ourselves. When Grace occurs something happens that is beautiful.

This book is an invocation to the possibility of such spiritual experiences and life altering and enlivening changes. This book seeks to do this in several ways. First, it opens us to the possibility of a micro-spiritual experience each day by a practice of an interactive daily meditation. Secondly, this book outlines a double awareness practice that invites Grace into our lives in a way that has been found to help reboot the brain system and allow us to change some of the old brain architecture that no longer serves us. Finally, in the daily Beauty thankfulness practice we learn a way to physically ground ourselves in the Beauty of our own reality. In this practice we build up the capacity to feel safe in the world, to free ourselves of old defensive patterns that no longer serve us, and to deepen and enliven our connection with the Mystery and Beauty of the world.

Most of the world's religions have a tradition of pilgrimage. A time of leaving the ordinary routine of life and traveling for days or weeks to a holy site for renewal. What this book tries to do is to bring that tradition of pilgrimage within a daily practice. To move us back closer to the source of what grounds and connects us to our lives. This book is targeted to people preoccupied with busyness, who have chosen a life that seems full and open, but is very often by the manner in which it occurs defined, narrow and disconnected. What needs connecting is our spirit to something beyond us. We often use the term God as applying to the mysterious power we seek connection with that lies beyond cognitive understanding. All of history has sought a definition of that term, and this history fails most of us individually time and again. For some of us, it may be the force that makes camellias bloom in winter, or the God of the Koran, or the explanation for quantum mechanics. If we are caught up in debating others' definitions and finding them failing it is a disconnection, a defense that may be preventing us from moving into what we feel, from risking belief and having faith, and from coming to terms with how to connect with the experience of our beliefs and faith and bring them into action in our lives.

Or, if we are like many others, it may be that the definition of God simply does not matter. If so, then we are already at the starting point to move beyond labels and definitions into a richer experience and deeper connection. For some of us it may help to think not of God at all but simply to think of Beauty. Beauty escapes the implications of theology. Beauty as I use the term is not an aesthetic intellectual exercise, but an aesthetic experience. Beauty is not a matter of faith or belief, but a practical and common experience. Beauty is a process of connection to something outside ourselves and connection to others who are also experiencing that connection. What we understand to be the experience of Beauty is in part the same as the more encompassing experience called God. God and Beauty are nouns, but as used in this book they are to be experienced as verbs.

How To Use This Book

This book seeks to inspire the possibility of greater connection with self, Beauty and others in several different ways:

- Meditations and image
- Reflection and further reflection
- Connection with the patterns of the seasons
- Holding a double awareness that invites Grace
- Daily Beauty thankfulness practice
- Daily assessment of connection practice
- Daily Examine/Inventory

Meditations and Image

This book is not meant to be a how-to book, although it has much practical advice. This book is intended to be a point of departure for reflective engagement with ourselves and with what is greater than us - for what we long for, for what we find beautiful. We start with the proposition that to just engage intellectually as the observer in what a more deeply lived life would be like is at best difficult, or at worst simply vicarious entertainment. Intellectual observation alone will not improve our lives and might even be regressive. So the words in the meditations are a process – they are to be assimilated and felt not just heard or seen in our heads. Where they might be felt in our bodies might be the bravest starting point. The images are to complement this movement out of the more rational left brain, into a more whole brain integrated bodily experience. The purpose of the words and images is not to give us knowledge as much as to open up the possibility of a deeper experience of ourselves and the world. Some of the meditation texts focus on an idea for only one day. Others attempt to mine a particular topic over several days, or a week or two.

The purpose of this variety in presentation is to keep the meditation experience fresh each day so that one day might be more thought-provoking and another more emotionally provoking. Overall the variety in presentation challenges us to have a more integrated experience of ourselves in which we discern throughout the texts and images our spiritual thread of connection.

The daily meditations are intended to affect the eighteen inch drop from the head to the heart. They do this by being more reflective than discursive, through image as much as words, and by relying more on poetic imagery than the prosaic. Still this book has the limitations of the print and image medium, and the imaginative use of these meditations is the key to their enrichment. The reader is encouraged to linger over each meditation text and image - to read the meditation for the day not like a textbook, but like a vase of flowers. We might read the meditations several times as if we were reading with the peripheral vision and not directly, so that meaning might emerge rather than be deduced, so that the images of each meditation may be absorbed into the heart.

Reflection and Further Reflection

The meditation book is designed to be laid open on a writing surface, so that facing pages can be seen and worked with. Following the text on each of these two facing pages is a heading Reflections. Under this heading is a space for the reader to write in response to both the meditation text and the meditation image for that day. Here dear reader you will dance with the writer and the photographers. Here you are invited to open your heart and mind to respond as fully and deeply as you can in response to the text and image.

Near the end of the space for writing your interactive response on the two facing pages is another heading called Further Reflection. This section begins with a question designed to take you deeper into your response to the text and image. The further reflection questions provide a starting point for a deeper daily examination of our lives. The further reflection question will be important to you if you did not have an initial response to the text and image. Or, it will serve you, if regardless of your response, the further reflection question opens up an additional avenue of response for you. Because of space limitations there is not space allocated for you to write in the meditation book in response to the further reflection question. You will want to use your own journal to respond to it.

One suggestion is to read a meditation and study the image in the morning and respond with your reflections. Then in the evening, the meditation text might be reread and the image again studied with a further reflections response centered upon an examination of the effect of the meditation on one's life that day. Any bodily engagement beyond just reading, meditating and writing is encouraged, and could yield even more sustenance: interacting with the text or image by dancing, body prayer, singing, drawing, painting or walking.

Connection with the Patterns of the Seasons

This book follows a seasonal calendar, because we are intimately connected with the flow of the seasons, and the seasons offer opportunities for deeper learning through their natural evolution. Before each seasonal section, questions are set out for you to add to the interactive meditation process during that season. Space is not allocated in the meditation book for you to respond to these seasonal questions and you will need to use your own journal in response to them. Please refer to these regularly doing each season.

During a given season you may want to focus on staying with one or two seasonal questions for a week at a time. This invites a process that allows the questions to open us to a deeper experience of the reality of our lives. One precaution, we need to be aware that a question may trigger a critical voice in our heads. We should acknowledge the voice, but not let it control. The purpose of our practices is to move deeper into our humanness and not to get trapped in critical judgment, which is a mental response that keeps us separated from our experience.

Holding a Double Awareness that Invites Grace

This meditation book also offers the chance to break down old patterns that have gotten wired into our brains that no longer serve us. This opportunity occurs when our reflections put us in touch emotionally with such nonproductive patterns. We may be in the grief of ending a relationship and realize we always do something to prevent ourselves from getting close to another person. We may recognize an underlying pattern in which we sabotage relationships to keep us safe from being hurt. The old pattern operates in our reptilian and limbic brains. There is no communication with our neo-cortex that tells us this pattern no longer serves our well-being. We can intervene on the old unconscious pattern by bringing to consciousness the old feeling that our journaling has caused us to re-experience (but not by re-triggering into the old trauma itself) and at the same time bringing to conscious awareness an experience of Beauty (e.g. a time when we felt close to the Beauty of nature or when we felt the Beauty of being loved without fear by a grandmother). We simply hold ourselves open to the possibility of Grace as we hold these two emotional experiences – one of wounding and one of healing in our felt awareness. If we can stay with this double awareness, often a shift will occur, sometimes small, sometimes large and permanent, in how our brains process such experiences. The experience of Beauty will in some way dissolve, modify or attenuate the capacity of the old wounding incident to control our present experience.

Daily Beauty Thankfulness Practice

Each day this meditation book offers the chance for us to write down several things we are grateful for that allow us to experience Beauty in our lives. The practice of gratitude cuts through old emotional reactive patterns like a finely sharpened blade. We write our gratitude list from a place of inner connection.

We achieve a place of inner connection to write our gratitude list from as follows:

- begin by taking a deep breath and closing your eyes
- relax your jaw
- take two more deep breaths
- as you let your breath out the third time, open your eyes slightly in the de-focused way
- bring your attention to your peripheral vision
- continue to breathe deeply and naturally and keep your attention on your peripheral vision
- bring your own awareness on what is around you -- what you hear, see, smell, the air on your skin
- ground yourself in the sensate world
- let your eyes smile
- then open your eyes fully and write your Beauty thankfulness list

Assessment of Connection Practice

For each day you will find a space to assess your level of connection to:

Self

Purpose

Mystery/Beauty

This is an awareness practice. Your connection to self is first of all a physical inquiry. Am I aware of feelings and sensations in my body? What are my emotions, my mood? Do I sense my energy and vitality? Are there places where aliveness in my body seems blocked? Often there are such areas, and the very act of bringing attention to them will restore greater blood flow and more aliveness. The other place to practice awareness of self is around what particular story we are living in. Am I aware of the story I am in this day? Is it a story of gratitude or a story of deprivation? Is it an old story that no longer serves me, or is it a new story with greater meaning? Am I moving between different stories? Ultimately this inquiry is about what is the nature of the experience of the self without having a story. Can I experience myself without a story? Who is that self?

The second part of the connection process is to connect with our purpose. Our actions follow our intentions. If we articulate our purpose each day, we are more likely to live in what that intention creates. My purpose might be to stay sober today. Or it might be to extend myself more into the world in some way. Or, it might be to do an act of kindness to a stranger. We are always in the process of changing and becoming. It is impossible to live a vital and fulfilling life with a deferred purpose. If we courageously commit ourselves to a daily purpose over and over again, gradually a reliance on our purpose grows. The practice of being intentional in our life builds up a reservoir of commitment to ourselves that is available when we face an opportunity to step into a greater experience of life.

The third part of the connection process is to sense our connection with the Mystery and Beauty of life. We each connect to the presence of a greater reality in different ways but there are common methods. Most useful are: practices of meditation, awareness of breathing, prayer, being in nature, journaling, an interactive meditation book like this, yoga, dance, chanting, etc.

You will want to use this book to explore the practices that are most helpful to you. But before you put practices to work in your life you first must be aware of your level of awareness of connection to Mystery and Beauty. The photographic images of this book are often of commonplace things. What makes these images powerful is the way the two talented photographers saw the images. The perspective of the photographer involves a larger reality. Similarly, it is our particular perspective on life that allows us entry into seeing the Mystery and Beauty of all life around us. As we exercise awareness on a daily basis, we become more alive to Mystery and Beauty.

Daily Examine/Inventory

At the end of this book, in the Appendix, you will find a Daily Examine/Inventory. A daily examination of one's life has been the hallmark of programs seeking to actualize human potential from the 16th century mystic St. Ignatius' twice daily examination of conscience to the tenth step of Alcoholics Anonymous' Twelve Steps. A series of daily questions is provided as a starting point. You will want to add questions to it that arise from your interaction with the meditations to personalize your own daily examination. The practice of daily examination is one that virtually guarantees progress on the spiritual journey.

In addition, Part Two of the Daily Examine/Inventory Appendix provides an awareness, acceptance and action practice for when you are stuck in emotional distress. The practice is a series of questions that provide insight into any emotional discomfort in which you are stuck. This section should be used at any time it might be helpful.

Conclusion

As you can see this interactive meditation book is a bit like a Swiss Army knife. It has many tools designed to aid you in your spiritual journey conveniently tucked into it. You need not use all of the tools that it offers at one time, but they are available for you when you need them. Start at whatever level meets the needs and motivation you have now, and come back frequently to the How To Use This Book section to remind yourself of all the possible tools available for your use. Now turn the page to today's date and let the Beauty of your spiritual journey began to unfold.

Photographer's Page

Photographs appearing on the following pages are copyright Ann Ehringhaus:

Seasonal Color Photo

March 22, 23, 26, 28-31

April 1-9, 11, 14-24, 28-31

May 1, 2, 4, 8, 16, 18, 20, 21, 23, 25-31

June 1-3, 5-9, 11, 13, 19, 20

To learn more about Ann Ehringhaus go to www.annehringhaus.com

Photographs appearing on the following pages are copyright Wayne Morris:

March 21, 24, 25, 27

April 10, 12, 13, 25

May 3, 5-7, 9-15, 17, 19, 22, 24

June 4, 10, 12

To learn more about Wayne Morris Photography go to www.wmphoto.biz

All photographs are printed with permission.

Spring – Renewal, Rebirth

Spring Questions

1. What is the deepest longing in my life?

2. Where in the darkest part of life might the greatest treasure grow?

3. Can I stay with and nurture what is hidden?

4. How am I most naturally creative in the world?

5. What new pattern is emerging in my life?

6. What nourishes me?

7. How am I becoming more whole?

8. How can I more deeply commit to the Mystery that is pulling me out of the ground into a new life?

9. What are the blessings I bring into the world?

10. How do I celebrate Beauty?

After a Long Winter

Spring Solstice. Up
early.

A restless night. Day
breaks gray.

A greenish haze is in
the tree tops.

In the uppermost
reaches of one large
oak,

a hundred feet off the
ground

where the new bud
green is thickest,

oblivious to height, to
the skinny

branches a lone
squirrel

hangs off the edge of
the world,

gathering the tender
fresh shoots, without
even

a sunrise's fanfare, a
working-class

yeoman gray squirrel
in the middle
kingdom

of an old yard, the ancient
treasure
the first piquant taste.

<u>Reflections:</u>

<u>Further Reflection</u>

What is the mysterious flavor that is awakening my life?

<u>Gratitude</u>

What am I thankful for that will allow me to experience Beauty in my life today?
1.
2.
3.

<u>Awareness of Connection</u>

	Low 1	2	3	4	5	6	7	8	9	High 10
To Self:										
To Purpose:										
To Mystery/Beauty:										

March 22

"Tell me the landscape in which you live and I will tell you who you are." Ortega y Gasset

A bit of the late winter flu bug has been going around. Lying in bed, in and out of sleep all afternoon, I awake to the pattern of bare limbs against the dome of bluest sky outside my window. The place I live, as it is with most of us, is ordinary. Yet at times our places seem to consciously be participating with us in life in an animate way. Ortega y Gasset reminds us that we interact with place. We do this whether or not we are aware of place's impact upon us.

In America, there are still huge amounts of space where no one lives. These spaces shape our psyches. These are wild places. We are heirs to a feeling of restlessness that prompts exploration. We move to try to find a new space that will give us a sense of discovery or of coming home or both. Anyone who has lived in a house more than a hundred years old can attest to the fact that we sometimes live trapped in spaces that dominate our lives. We are constantly interacting with place in a way to try to learn more of who we are. And we often wish to surrender to some "place-ness" outside ourselves that seems to know more who we are than we do.

Reflections:

Further Reflection

How does the place I live in shape me?

Gratitude

What am I thankful for that will allow me to experience Beauty in my life today?
1.
2.
3.

Awareness of Connection

	Low									High
	1	2	3	4	5	6	7	8	9	10

To Self:
To Purpose:
To Mystery/Beauty:

March 23

The Medicine Wheel atop Medicine Mountain in Wyoming, Stonehenge, Jerusalem, and many other places are sacred places that function in a special way within the human imagination. A place like Medicine Wheel attracts not only tourists and Native Americans from dozens of different tribes to perform ceremonies that are magnified by being in this place, but also New Age enthusiasts searching for vortex points of electromagnetic energy, artists drawn to the sweep of wildflowers on the windswept slopes and naturalists drawn to the imagery of the relentless view to the horizon. How do we discover a relationship to place that moves beyond a naïveté that sees place as wholly magical, that does not deny the scientific reductionism of our age, to an experience that deepens our sense of wonder, mystery and meaning?

This is not an academic question. In the abstract any answer that has not been experienced will always be confusing. As the question suggests, the answer only comes from experiencing sacred space.

Reflections:

Further Reflection

Where on this earth am I drawn in order to experience more fully who I am? Where in the natural world am I drawn to more fully experience greater consciousness?

Gratitude
What am I thankful for that will allow me to experience Beauty in my life today?
1.
2.
3.

Awareness of Connection

	Low									High
	1	2	3	4	5	6	7	8	9	10
To Self:										
To Purpose:										
To Mystery/Beauty:										

March 24

What determines the cultural feel of San Francisco, New York, or London is the spirit of the place. Urban spaces are combinations of natural and man created space. All great cities feel uniquely themselves. A guide book can try to describe the differences in descriptive, touristy language and miss precisely what the spirit is. But we know immediately when we visit and experience it.

What is the spirit of the place in which we live that we take for granted? Do we live unconscious of the spirit of the place in which we live day to day? Does the spirit of our place move us more into our authentic life, or does the spirit of our place fight with who we might most want to become?

Reflections:

Further Reflection

What is the spirit of the place I live in? Does it call me forth?

Gratitude

What am I thankful for that will allow me to experience Beauty in my life today?

1.
2.
3.

Awareness of Connection

	Low									High
	1	2	3	4	5	6	7	8	9	10
To Self:										
To Purpose:										
To Mystery/Beauty:										

March 25

Last night it thundered and snowed. The wet snow clung to everything. This morning all the confusion of twigs, limbs and branches that are taken for granted were revealed in dazzling white. All was a soft quietness in an insulated world. A blue sky capped a white wonderland.

This dramatic change of weather in late winter, heralded by trumpets of thunder, is magical. The change in the outer world has the capacity to change our inner perspective. Our inner perspective can be the same old pattern of how life, the world, are supposed to be or should be. Then suddenly in winter it thunders and snows and all is not as we would think it is. The undefined browns and grays of winter are suddenly pure crystalline white.

The weather opens up a new perspective on our world – a fairy land, a landscape of infinite imagination, a place of surprise. It is almost impossible to imagine our lives changing to the same degree, as rapidly as the world outside has changed. Yet it is just as possible. We choose the way we experience life by the perspective we have about life. If we are open to the possibility of seeing a hawk on the way home tonight, we are much more likely to see one because of our openness to the possibility.

Reflections:

Further Reflection

What would it mean to be open to the possibility of thunder and snow in my life? What is the snow I long for? What is the thunder?

Gratitude

What am I thankful for that will allow me to experience Beauty in my life today?
1.
2.
3.

Awareness of Connection

	Low									High
	1	2	3	4	5	6	7	8	9	10
To Self:										
To Purpose:										
To Mystery/Beauty:										

March 26

Snow and thunder weather remind us that unexpectedly a new truth can be revealed. We don't think that thunder and lightning accompany a snow storm. Yet yesterday's weather revealed they can.

In 1854 everyone thought that cholera was caused by the dreaded smells from the uncontrolled pollution and open sewers of Victorian London. One man, John Snow, looked for truth in what did not seem obvious and found the source of the cholera outbreak in the water at the Broad Street pump.

What is urgent may not be important. What is obvious may not be true. Our brains work by creating patterns and then pushing sensory data into these patterns. Sometimes the data fits, sometimes it does not.

We have to take a stand against our pattern-adapting brains. We have to offset the efficiency of this patterning process by realizing that it may throw us into small or serious error. We have to develop some process to assess the helpfulness of our spontaneous patterning assessments.

Buddhism is the oldest tradition that has focused on how the mind works. Aware of the dangers of the brain patterning process, Buddhist teachers recommend a practice that serves as a counterweight called "Beginner's Mind." Simply put, they recommend that we constantly try to see things afresh. This practice allows us again and again to return to the possibility of seeing something new as opposed to imposing an old pattern on new data. We have the possibility of seeing a relationship in a new light, a job from a new perspective, or experiencing healing where there only seemed to be loss.

Reflections:

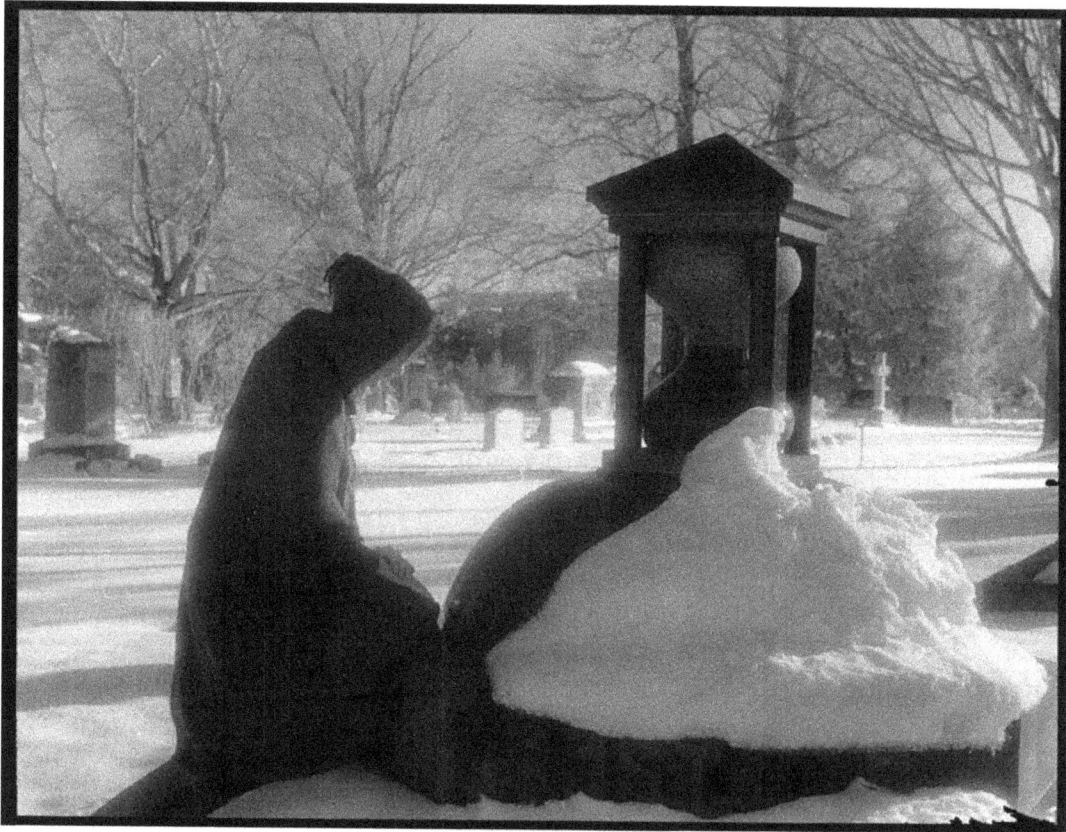

Further Reflection

Where in my life do I need to have a beginner's perspective?

Gratitude

What am I thankful for that will allow me to experience Beauty in my life today?

1.
2.
3.

Awareness of Connection

	Low									High	
	1	2	3	4	5	6	7	8	9	10	

To Self:

To Purpose:

To Mystery/Beauty:

March 27

The brain's patterning process can prevent us from seeing what is real. We have all heard the old saw: "Truth is stranger than fiction." A contemporary phrase is – "Get Real." As these catch phrases suggest, there is a part of us that thirsts to get beyond how this or that pattern appears which is often labeled good or bad, to what is always more intriguing – what is real.

Realism is seeing things as they really are. It is the opposite of both pessimism and optimism.

The first cousin of realistic thinking is curiosity. Together, "being real" and being curious about what is real add up to a defense against tyranny, both psychological tyranny like addiction/depression and political tyranny – the obsession of one group in power that believes only it holds hope and truth. Both psychological tyranny and political tyranny are about a lack of trust, a failure to be open, to be curious. Both reify ideas at the expense of the material and spiritual.

Reflections:

16

Further Reflection
Where do I delude myself by attachment to an idea and I fail to see what is real?
Gratitude
What am I thankful for that will allow me to experience Beauty in my life today?
1.
2.
3.

Awareness of Connection

	Low									High
	1	2	3	4	5	6	7	8	9	10
To Self:										
To Purpose:										
To Mystery/Beauty:										

March 28

If we view life realistically, we see that life is dangerous and often extraordinarily difficult. We also see that though life can seem overwhelmingly weighty does not mean it is best to live life all that seriously. The conflict of these two ideas is only resolved in how we live life.

The challenge of the life of the mind – similar to the challenge of the life of the heart or the body – is to love ideas and know their limitations. To be aware that when our ideas take us too far from what our heart values or what is curious in the material world, we have become like a great empty library where no one ever checks out a book.

When we get too far away from the material and our heart, we lose our humility. When we are in touch with our humility we stay grounded in a dignity that acknowledges acceptance of our dependency upon and interaction with the rest of the world.

Reflections:

Further Reflection

Do my ideas about life take me out of living my life?

Gratitude

What am I thankful for that will allow me to experience Beauty in my life today?
1.
2.
3.

Awareness of Connection

	Low									High
	1	2	3	4	5	6	7	8	9	10
To Self:										
To Purpose:										
To Mystery/Beauty:										

March 29

This morning is warm. The night's slow rain stopped at dawn, and, as the air clears, sunlight sparkles in the trees. At a contemplative service last night, I was sitting in the quiet, a banquet of candles flickering in the center of the circle and something shifted. I was no longer in competition with the world, or even my own thoughts and feelings. I was no longer the person who had to figure it out, get it right, or make sure life happened in a certain way – everything, as it is, was enough. I experienced a moment of Grace.

Grace is often not as obvious in our lives as many of the themes in these meditations: having a positive outlook, seeing the world realistically, being less judgmental, having patience, being curious, and above all being at peace – and how these themes integrated.

But utilizing practices that bring these themes more into our lives, opens us up to the unexpected, dramatic way change can occur that we call Grace.

We have all had such moments. The challenge is to recognize this gold. To return again and again to the nuggets of emotional ore when we are set free. We can forget, minimize, or rationalize the strokes of Grace in our lives, or we can strive to take them with us in our emotional memory to restart the centering we need when our lives are off-center and out of balance.

We often use emotional memory to carry memories of fear and defensive reactions. We can also use our emotional memory to carry seeds of vitality, love and presence.

The former occurs out of our hard wiring for survival. The latter occurs because we become skilled in tapping our richest emotional wellsprings, the spots of Grace in our lives.

Reflections:

Further Reflection

How may I live more from an openness to Grace?

Gratitude

What am I thankful for that will allow me to experience Beauty in my life today?
1.
2.
3.

Awareness of Connection

	Low									High
	1	2	3	4	5	6	7	8	9	10
To Self:										
To Purpose:										
To Mystery/Beauty:										

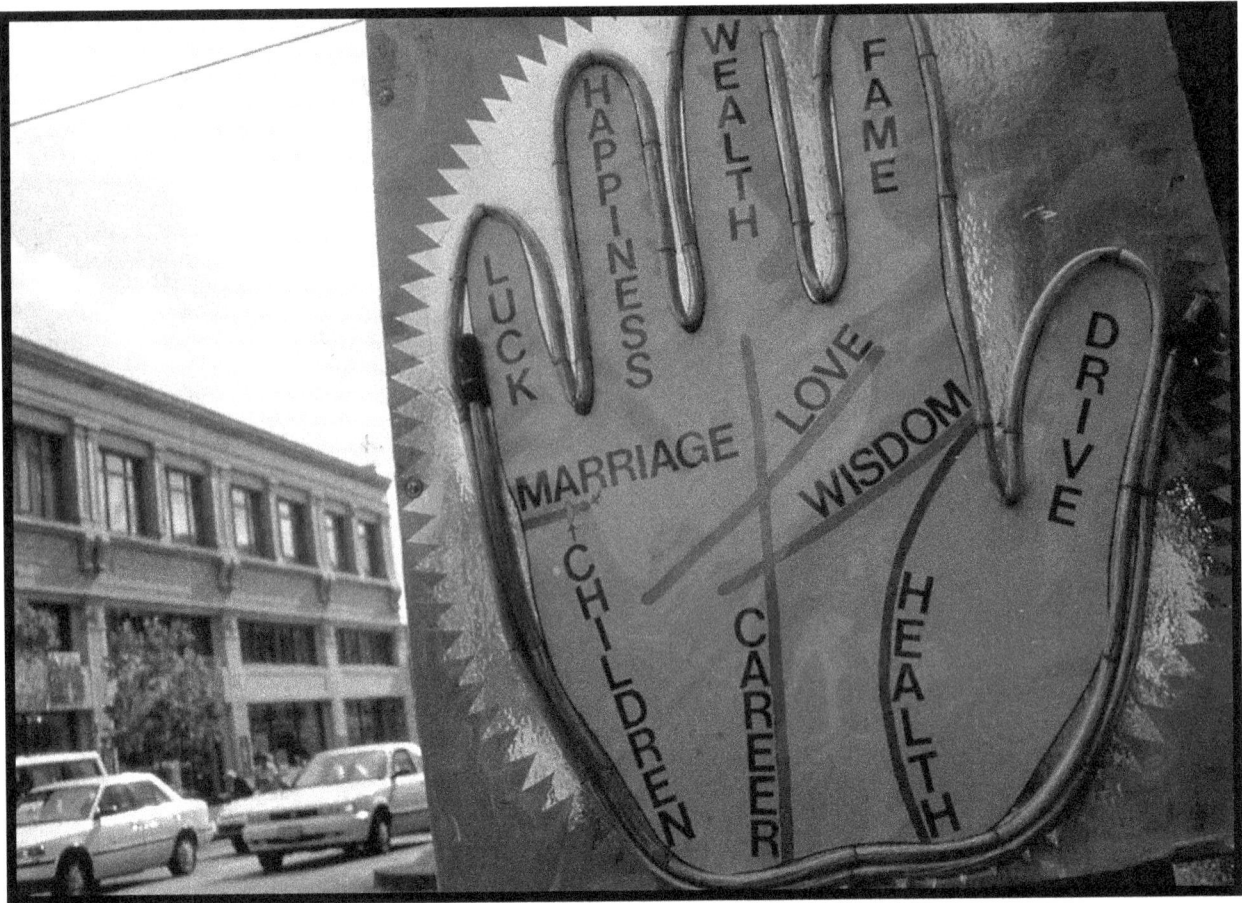

Grace always surprises. An example is the experience of Amy Sutherland, a journalist reporting on her experience observing techniques for training killer whales like Shamu.

The trainers start from the obvious premise that you can neither forcibly move nor dominate a killer whale. Whether we wish to be simply courteous or just realistic, this is a premise we should have in our interaction with other humans.

The simple rule of such animal training is reward the behavior you want and ignore the behavior you don't like. The former requires you to be proactive – and, in more human terms, to make love an action word. The latter requires that one great and often illusive characteristic of maturity, patience.

The animal trainer knows that in all interaction with others, we are teaching them how to treat us. There is no recess. School is always relentlessly in session. But even though school is always open we come with a bias, we don't like the idea of training. Training reminds us of school. Or we consider the idea of training others as demeaning, not our place or discourteous.

Animal trainers don't get caught up in these worries – they know all interactions with their animals are training sessions. This reality is the same for human interactions.

The human corollary to the animal training axiom of ignoring bad behavior is not to be overly sensitive. We don't get our feelings hurt when a whale's behavior is erratic. Patience is about giving humans the same break. Love and patience are the ground out of which the surprise of Grace is most likely to come.

Reflections:

<table>
<tr><td colspan="11">

<u>Further Reflection</u>
Where am I "training" others to treat me in a manner I don't like?

<u>Gratitude</u>
What am I thankful for that will allow me to experience Beauty in my life today?
1.
2.
3.

<u>Awareness of Connection</u>
</td></tr>
</table>

	Low									High
	1	2	3	4	5	6	7	8	9	10
To Self:										
To Purpose:										
To Mystery/Beauty:										

March 31

Applying animal training lessons to humans helps us recognize that our behavior is often a more efficient medium of communication than language.

Animal trainers think of behavior communication just as behavior – it is neither right nor wrong, about caring or not caring, about being smart or dumb.

This means that animal trainers don't get upset or angry over behavior they don't like. For humans this means not nagging another about behavior you don't like. None of us like to nag, or be nagged, and for the most part nagging doesn't work – what it does do is deflate the mood of both people.

Nagging is a poor option. What works is positively reinforcing the behavior you want.

All animal training works better when the animal is having fun. So we need not reinforce positive behavior in an authoritarian way, or from a hierarchical position.

Give easily and freely and the animal, or the other human being we want in our life, will usually give freely in return.

Strikingly, Sutherland admits that the information she is providing in her book will probably not help you create the relationship life you want. The information only impacted her because of her experience over time of seeing it work with animals and then practicing it herself with others. Her admission is the challenging reminder that only by sustained experiencing of new patterns of behavior do we reach the emotional reward that reinforces them.

Reflections:

Further Reflection

Am I willing to practice new behavior that will allow me to experience the emotional pay-off of teaching others a positive way to treat me?

Gratitude

What am I thankful for that will allow me to experience Beauty in my life today?
1.
2.
3.

Awareness of Connection

Low									High
1	2	3	4	5	6	7	8	9	10

To Self:
To Purpose:
To Mystery/Beauty:

April 1

If we decide to give up nagging, and being verbally judgmental, how do we use positive reinforcement to strengthen our relationships?

First, we must be curious enough to see what is reinforcing to another. Then timing becomes important. Once we observe desired behavior, the time to reinforce it is immediately.

A corollary to reinforcing desired behavior is that trying does not count. As Obe-Wan told Luke Skywalker: "No try, just do." Trying among humans often translates into talking about the new behavior and dissipating part of the energy actually needed to achieve something new. How often have you talked with someone about quitting smoking or losing weight. Trying includes self doubt about the possibility of success.

But while trying does not count, baby steps do. We want problems solved immediately, and old behaviors formed over dozens of years are not transformed in a day.

An important lesson from animal trainers is patience. Figure out simple steps that lead to the outcome you desire and reinforce as each is learned and becomes incorporated into routine behavior.

The lessons of animal training boil down to our need for patience, our need to practice new behavior when we want a new outcome, and respect for the dignity of another.

<u>Reflections:</u>

<u>Further Reflection</u>
Am I more interested in changing another than changing myself?

<u>Gratitude</u>
What am I thankful for that will allow me to experience Beauty in my life today?
1.
2.
3.

<u>Awareness of Connection</u>

	Low									High
	1	2	3	4	5	6	7	8	9	10
To Self:										
To Purpose:										
To Mystery/Beauty:										

April 2

At Sea World in the 1980's, the animal trainers developed a technique known as Least Reinforcing Scenario (LRS). This is a way for the trainer to tell the animal its behavior is wrong without giving the behavior so much attention it actually reinforces the behavior.

LRS is a pause, a non-response. It requires one to not be caught up in the behavior of another (in other words not to fuel that behavior) and at the same time not to get triggered by the other emotionally.

If the dolphin does something wrong – for example squirts water when signaled to move a fin – the trainer doesn't bat an eye, she simply stands still for a few beats, no sounds, no sighs and then resumes training.

Apply this to our best friend or spouse's most irritating behavior. Our spouse becomes angry because the computer is not working. We don't respond, we don't get triggered into negative behavior and we don't ignore. After the pause, we go on as before.

The LRS is a practice of not letting what is outside us control how our insides are. At first it will be hard, but the rewards are very reinforcing. We are taking charge of our lives. We are letting go of old stories we have around others' behavior patterns. The new story is about what serves our equanimity and peace of mind.

Reflections:

Further Reflection

How can I put LRS's to use in my life? What values might be served?

Gratitude

What am I thankful for that will allow me to experience Beauty in my life today?

1.

2.

3.

Awareness of Connection

	Low									High
	1	2	3	4	5	6	7	8	9	10

To Self:

To Purpose:

To Mystery/Beauty:

April 3

In addition to teaching new tricks, animal trainers often work to change a behavior that is not helpful. They don't try to change the old behavior, rather they teach a new behavior that is incompatible with the old behavior.

This approach resembles the martial arts approach of blending with an adversary. It is much more difficult to stop a punch coming at us than to blend with the attacker's energy and use it to throw the attacker.

Similarly, we all have unconscious patterns of energy that create behaviors we don't like. The solution is to engage the energy in a task that is incompatible with what is not desired. Trainers had the problem that two spotted eagle rays were nipping at the divers when they got in the tank to feed them. This behavior emerged from the divers feeding the rays by hand. So the divers developed a new way of feeding the rays using a little PVC pipe tray. The rays stopped nipping as they focused their energy on opening their new lunch box.

We can try this on ourselves – if we engage in some behavior that is not helpful, like going to the grocery store hungry and buying more than we need – then practice eating a snack before shopping. Develop a pattern of behavior incompatible with behavior that reinforces outcomes you don't value.

Reflections:

<u>Further Reflection</u>
Is there a pattern of behavior I can change easily by harnessing the energy in a different direction?

<u>Gratitude</u>
What am I thankful for that will allow me to experience Beauty in my life today?
1.
2.
3.

<u>Awareness of Connection</u>

	Low									High
	1	2	3	4	5	6	7	8	9	10
To Self:										
To Purpose:										
To Mystery/Beauty:										

April 4

A psychological and spiritual reality is that estrangement – from self, others, purpose, Beauty, Mystery – aggravates or encourages mental-illnesses, addiction and general unhappiness.

All of these connections are important, but connection to self is one of the most complicated. Sometimes out of a quest for safety and security, we let go of a dream, or a part of ourselves, and for the rest of our lives something is missing. The longing we failed to embrace leads in mid-life to a sense of failure no matter what our outward success. Depression comes easily.

The answer is to go back and re-connect with the lost dream, to give it some room in our life. In youth, the dream might have been overwhelming – the desire to be a race car driver or a full time novelist. In maturity, we can become a serious race fan or we can find a meaningful outlet for our desire to write.

Reflections:

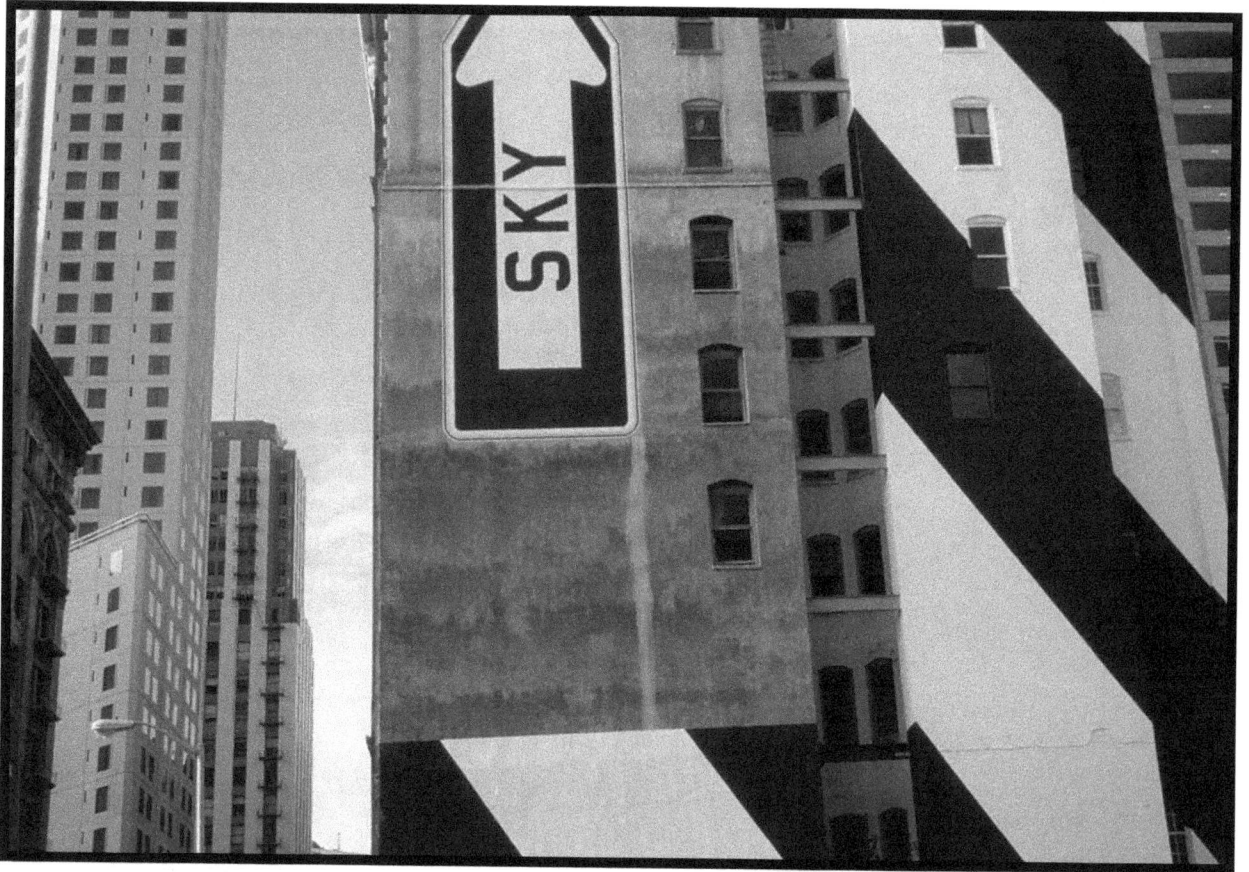

What is that neglected part like?

Gratitude

What am I thankful for that will allow me to experience Beauty in my life today?

1.
2.
3.

Awareness of Connection

	Low									High
	1	2	3	4	5	6	7	8	9	10

To Self:

To Purpose:

To Mystery/Beauty:

April 5

Opposite the difficulty of neglecting a part of who we are is the problem of having too great an identification with who we think we are. We can become so attached to a dream or an idea of who we are that we become blind to realities – to what is presently in front of us to be enjoyed and nurtured.

We are aware of how we can be attached to ways of avoiding life – e.g. attached to a perspective of poor me, a self-pity perspective, or attached to the use of alcohol (addiction) in order not to feel difficult emotions. Our psyches are complex energy bundles – we are lots of things. Attachment to a monolithic idea of self can ironically be a source of dis-connection. But in addition to attachment to avoiding emotions, or a limiting perception, we can be attached to an idea of who we think we are, or who we think we should be.

The underlying unity of self is experienced when we live fully committed to an authentic experience of self and also do not cling too tightly to what the self is – that is, we stay curious about the stories we tell ourselves of who we are.

From this perspective the energy of life, our life force, flows most freely.

Reflections:

Further Reflection

Is there a part of my life I am overly attached to? What is that about?

Gratitude

What am I thankful for that will allow me to experience Beauty in my life today?
1.
2.
3.

Awareness of Connection

	Low									High
	1	2	3	4	5	6	7	8	9	10
To Self:										
To Purpose:										
To Mystery/Beauty:										

April 6

"Choose love not fear." Seems easy, simplistic. But it is difficult and demanding.

A part of us hates the arbitrariness of such simple quotes to guide this complicated thing called life. Yet when we let go of our arrogance about the easy solution, we find that within the cliché is some truth we are withholding from ourselves. As this quote suggests, there is, at least for many of us, some fear that is not letting us live a whole life and is holding back part of our lives.

As always the problem is consciousness: How to be in the moment and also have enough consciousness of the moment to see if our own software is running fear or love.

We change our software by changing the patterns in our lives. What patterns must we change to run love, not fear? What would it mean to upgrade from love 1.0 to love 4.0?

Reflections:

Further Reflection

Today what would it mean in my life to run love 4.0 or higher?

Gratitude

What am I thankful for that will allow me to experience Beauty in my life today?

1.

2.

3.

Awareness of Connection

	Low									High
---	1	2	3	4	5	6	7	8	9	10
To Self:										
To Purpose:										
To Mystery/Beauty:										

April 7

A wonderful soaking rain has fallen all morning. The earth, like a young puppy alert that its owner is just beyond the door, is perked up and astir. The dampness and gray of the day juxtapose the excitement that lies just beneath the surface. Spring brings a new kind of Mystery, different from the dark Mystery of winter. Spring's Mystery is so abundant it almost seems not to be mysterious. While the changes of spring are obvious, the meaning of the excitement of our longing may be less clear. We may need to take time to be in the magic of springtime wonder and waiting.

Reflections:

Further Reflection

Where in my life is nature modeling a new opportunity for me?

Gratitude

What am I thankful for that will allow me to experience Beauty in my life today?
1.
2.
3.

Awareness of Connection

	Low									High
	1	2	3	4	5	6	7	8	9	10

To Self:
To Purpose:
To Mystery/Beauty:

April 8

We all remember from elementary school the kid who was fully emotionally present and whose emotional exuberance got him or her into trouble with the teachers. On the other hand were those good students who protected themselves by being emotionally reserved, who didn't get into trouble because their way of coping kept their emotions damped down.

By the time we are adults most of us have made some accommodation with our culture, a sort of unconscious bargain of how we must be in the world to be emotionally safe. And most of us, in making that bargain, gave up a good deal. We mixed up experiencing our feelings with expressing them, and because expressing them got us in trouble we internalized the message not to feel them.

Whatever the unconscious bargain, in order to live fully in the Mystery and Beauty of life, most of us need to reclaim or re-vitalize our emotional way of being in the world.

Some years back psychological theory made the mistake of referring to our inner emotional guidance system as the "inner child." This term is unfortunate because it allows the importance of our emotional core to be trivialized and it is an inadequate descriptive label of this part of the psyche.

What does have resonance in this label are the child-like qualities of our emotional core. It is this aspect that allows us to be over-sensitive and repeatedly wounded. It is also this aspect that carries our visa into Heaven, into the experience of feeling loved abundantly so that we are able to love selflessly.

Reflections:

Further Reflection

How can I live more fully from my emotional core?

Gratitude

What am I thankful for that will allow me to experience Beauty in my life today?

1.
2.
3.

Awareness of Connection

	Low									High
	1	2	3	4	5	6	7	8	9	10

To Self:

To Purpose:

To Mystery/Beauty:

April 9

We avoid our feelings by addictive processes – compulsive shopping or eating, manipulating or attempting to control. We avoid our feelings by trying to get over them – by telling ourselves we shouldn't feel however we feel, or by trying to transcend them by doing something "spiritual" and repressing our feelings.

Many of us live vicarious feeling lives, going to movies and weeping deeply over silver screen characters. We experience their feeling lives because we are afraid to live our own. Their feelings appear real in us because we are out of touch with our own. Many of us avoid our feelings because we are long out of practice at expressing them in positive ways and now we don't want to make a fool out of ourselves. The truth is, as we learn to be in touch with our feelings, we will occasionally look foolish. The great virtue of risking looking foolish is it brings a gentle humility.

Growing into emotional maturity starts with humility. We wish there were short cuts around feelings, or that feelings were simply not that important. But it is only through our anger, depression and despair that we learn when we are not taking good care of ourselves. It is only in our sadness, grief and loss we learn what we truly value. And it is only in our serenity, joy and enthusiasm we learn how to truly love.

Reflections:

Further Reflection

What are the strategies I employ to avoid my feelings? Are they worth it?

Gratitude

What am I thankful for that will allow me to experience Beauty in my life today?
1.
2.
3.

Awareness of Connection

	Low									High
	1	2	3	4	5	6	7	8	9	10
To Self:										
To Purpose:										
To Mystery/Beauty:										

April 10

Spring Anima

Redbud trees bring spring. They
are her first announcement – though
like many proclamations not
entirely true.

In March they begin stringing
tiny purple lights
direct upon the branches –
stems come later in April
on the blossoms.

A curious reversal,
going first for what mostly
should come later -
the ideal blooming
brilliantly in first blush.

Once in an inspiration I bought
a beautiful woman a round trip ticket
to Europe. Even today she doesn't know
Lufthansa lifted off one day
without her.

The ticket was non-refundable.
Redbuds fade, undetectable from the highway,
low undergrowth hardly noticed.

I have been tempted to cut
down the two redbuds in the yard.
But something is served by their early
secret longing,
their too quick grasp that never fills.

Young boys stumble into the Grail castle
and are dumbstruck, awake the next morning to
find the house deserted.

The redbud knight is off before dawn
charging into spring.

<u>Reflections:</u>

Still I love the purple kisses
gracefully tied to her supple branches.
Her urgent firstness. She asks over and over
again
each year, what does my Beauty
serve?

Two answers are possible:
Me – some childish need to stay stuck
in the warm fragrance of her poetry; and
God – an answer more complicated than
the question.

Do redbuds' Beauty serve us, as our inner
longing
for Beauty serves God?

Maybe No.
On this one March
redbud blessed day
likely not for a great cause,
nor a rush to create some new reality.

Maybe Yes. Right here in a small unheroic
way.

Spring's graceful redbud Beauty is served –
by time alone in the February wind
by gathering her flowers
by patience in the long summer
by being with silence
by looking into her eyes
by delighting in her sensuous Beauty, by do or
not do – no try….

The list expands
by more of those words used to march
deeper into the action verb, love.

What question is the redbud asking me today?

Gratitude
What am I thankful for that will allow me to experience Beauty in my life today?
1.
2.
3.

Awareness of Connection

	Low									High
	1	2	3	4	5	6	7	8	9	10

To Self:
To Purpose:
To Mystery/Beauty:

April 11

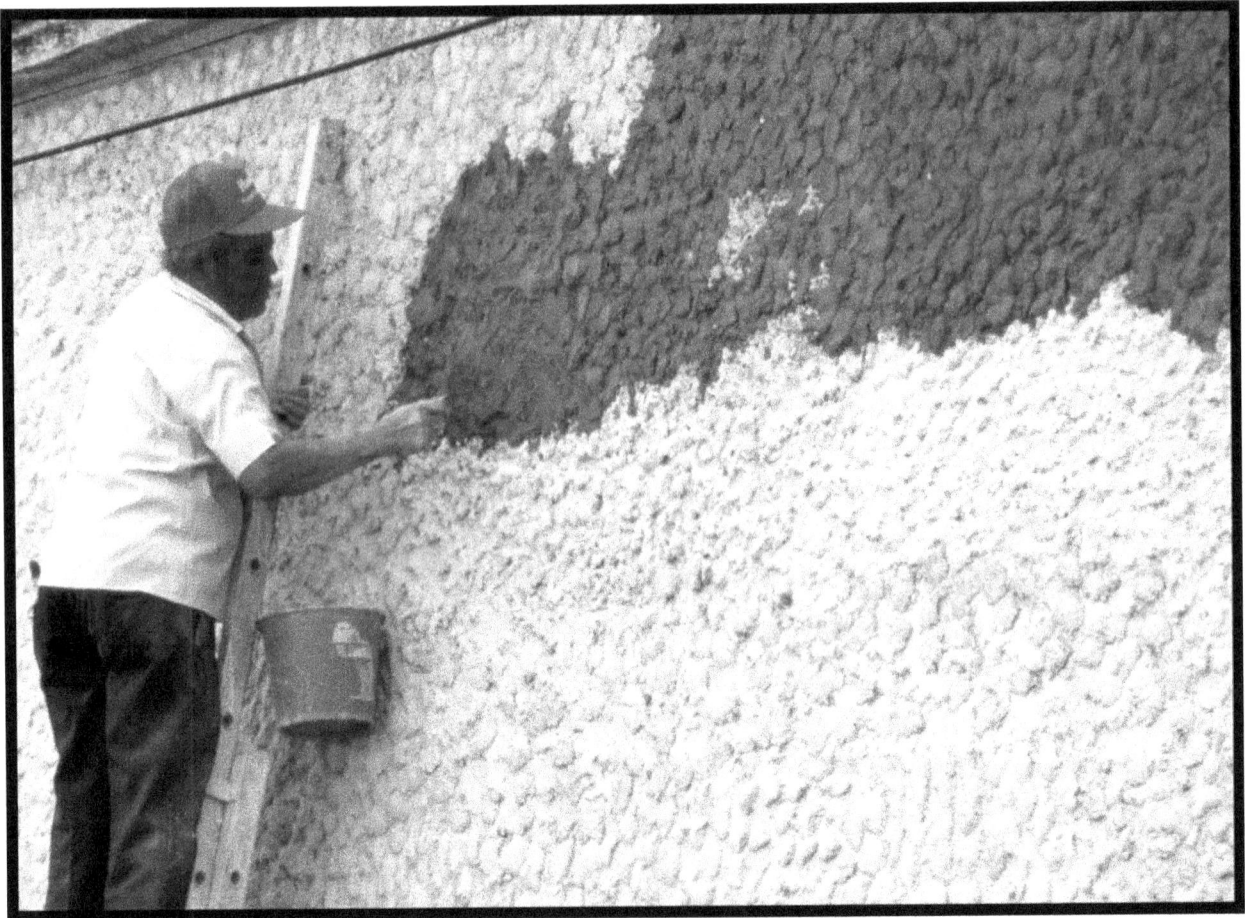

Those who have learned to live out of touch with their emotional core are out of touch with what helps connect and validate the connections we make to ourselves, others and God. Such a path of living cuts us off from Beauty.

There are two primary manifestations of this cut-offness. First, is the personality who has learned to put such a premium on safety that he holds back from a feeling experience of life. The other is the opposite – the person who gushes over with feelings and talking about feelings. This quick blow-off of feelings prevents the full experiencing of feelings just as surely as the feeling repressor.

In both cases, the feeling avoidance strategies are learned defenses to life – ways each personality creates a sense of safety in the world. Both strategies end up preventing what the strategy was initially devised to help achieve – a fuller, deeper experience of life.

Reflections:

Further Reflection

What are my strategies to help me avoid the experience of my emotional life?

Gratitude

What am I thankful for that will allow me to experience Beauty in my life today?
1.
2.
3.

Awareness of Connection

	Low									High	
	1	2	3	4	5	6	7	8	9	10
To Self:										
To Purpose:										
To Mystery/Beauty:										

April 12

Most of us begin adulthood wounded in some way, so we adopt protective strategies which, while they may be absolutely necessary at first, ultimately keep us disconnected from life. There are two ways we change from a person controlled by self-centered defensive strategies, to a person able to freely connect to self, others and God. Sometimes we are in such a place of pain and despair that we experience a sudden shift in our will, where we are cut loose from the ego's bonds of willfulness and become willing to learn a new way. It is the way of suffering, of "via negative," where if we survive, miraculously our lives turn in a new direction.

The other way is when we slowly learn to trust, and we slowly begin to build up a set of experiences that reinforces greater and greater trust.

The difficulty with the slow, positive approach is that initially our trust is weak making it difficult to take responsibility for the ways our old defensive patterns are creating our pain. We don't yet trust enough to take responsibility for a new perspective that brings joy and serenity. We don't yet have the emotional reinforcement from living in adult trust (that is, trust built on wise decisions and good boundaries). It is a catch-22. We only get trust by trusting, but we do not yet have the emotional reinforcement trusting brings. So we go slowly.

This is a difficult strategy for most of us, who want whatever we want now. But it is like averaging in when buying a stock – a cautious and prudent way to establish a new position.

Reflections:

	Further Reflection	

Further Reflection
What might I do to slowly build greater trust?

Gratitude
What am I thankful for that will allow me to experience Beauty in my life today?
1.
2.
3.

Awareness of Connection

	Low 1	2	3	4	5	6	7	8	9	High 10
To Self:										
To Purpose:										
To Mystery/Beauty:										

April 13

We learn pragmatically. We get safe and trustworthy people in our lives, and we begin to trust them. We pick a spiritual path and begin the discipline of prayer, meditation, devotion and service it offers in order to learn to experience trust in something greater than ourselves. There are two dangers. The first is we will reject a spiritual path because it comes bathed in a religion and religions inherently suffer from dogma and hypocrisy. However, we can miss a great vehicle to move deeper into the joy of life by letting our judgmental ego about religion run the show.

The second danger is that we will try to make a homemade vehicle for our spiritual journey. We invest a whole lot of ego in what the contours of our spiritual life are. This ego investment is exactly what will keep us from having the humility so essential for spiritual progress. Our homemade vehicle will probably not have the rigor, discipline and mentorship found in traditional spiritual paths. Or, it may be overly self-flagellating and carry the burden of ego found in the zealot.

Reflections:

	Further Reflection	

Further Reflection

What path am I on? Have I chosen it consciously and wisely?

Gratitude

What am I thankful for that will allow me to experience Beauty in my life today?
1.
2.
3.

Awareness of Connection

	Low									High	
	1	2	3	4	5	6	7	8	9	10	
To Self:											
To Purpose:											
To Mystery/Beauty:											

April 14

How

Spring's newborn wonder –

   this bright wet morning
slick from the womb of winter.

Purple rods of redbud,
   random dogwood fires
petals burning white,
   careless yellow ropes
tethering the tops of wherever
   jasmine reaches.

How to hope,
   as unbidden nature longs?

How to bury kin in bursting season?

How to love, when we know
   not what love is, or why, or if,
   we love –
when nothing green or the unfolding arms of color
   expresses any scintilla of doubt?
and how not.

Reflections:

Further Reflection

How may I live the life nature's Beauty models for me?

Gratitude

What am I thankful for that will allow me to experience Beauty in my life today?

1.

2.

3.

Awareness of Connection

	Low									High
	1	2	3	4	5	6	7	8	9	10

To Self:

To Purpose:

To Mystery/Beauty:

April 15

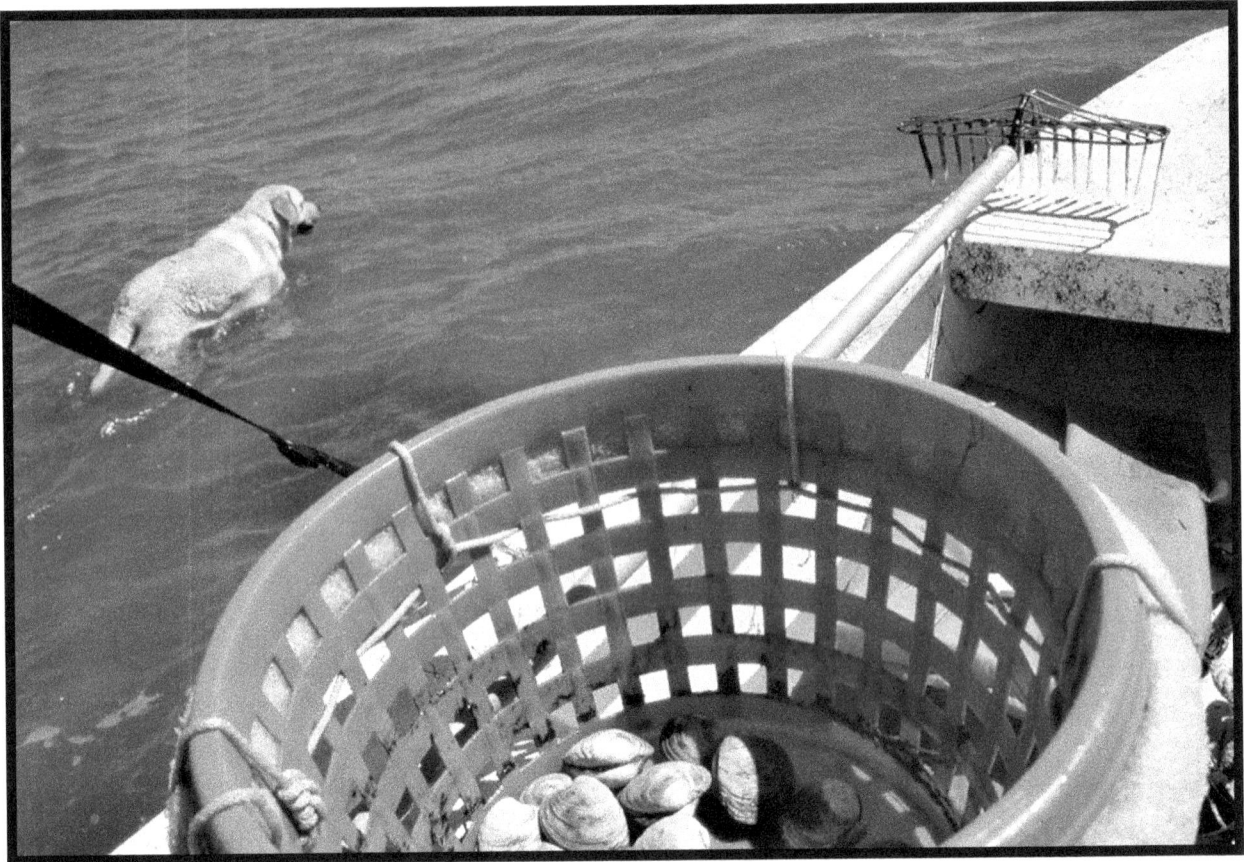

Render unto Caesar day. What is due to be rendered to whom, and for what, in our lives? Most of the time Caesar gets his. But do we hear the need to love, to be a friend, to be creative, to be open to receiving love, to laugh, to create joy? Do we hear these with the same attention as we hear the old tinny voice of Caeser?

No, we grant Caesar more authority in our lives than many more important things. We do this partially because these higher authorities set no deadlines of today. And because we don't want to disappoint ourselves.

We avoid disappointing ourselves by neglecting the steady practices that create the conditions for the demands of these higher authorities. When the foot work is not done, when the demands are not conscious, or even when they are, and the call of love, Beauty and creativity are ignored, then we befriend anger, resentment and cynicism.

Today we also have the opportunity to render unto love, to life, to creativity the weak tax they demand to run our beautiful country of an open, free and joyful life.

Reflections:

Further Reflection
Today how will I render unto life and love?
 	
 Gratitude
What am I thankful for that will allow me to experience Beauty in my life today?
1.
2.
3.
 	
 Awareness of Connection
           Low   High
           1   2   3   4   5   6   7   8   9   10
To Self:
To Purpose:
To Mystery/Beauty:

April 16

The easy cliché is: "One needs to be more authentic." As if that were a product we could pick up at the store. An illusion of moving toward a linear goal. Not so.

Authenticity is like springtime, a yearning pulls us deeper and deeper into life; it is not a place we get to until perhaps we let go of the idea of getting there.

What seems like a pull is often the pull to pseudo-authenticity. A pull toward wanting the world to embrace us in a way we want to be succored. This is not so much a pull into authenticity as a longing for an impossible reality, a reality that has everything childhood failed at – a longing for something that does not exist.

We must get past wanting the size ten world to fit our size eleven foot, without pinches and blisters, past the notion of getting to a bench where we can sit back or lie down.

Once we accept that the path always goes on, the shoe never fits the way we'd like – if we can surrender our preconception of the way things should be to the Mystery of life – then we get to wander barefoot through the thick new, green Grace of spring.

Reflections:

Further Reflection

How can I give up my limited ideas of how my life should be and humbly squeeze from the old rinds of doubt, the love juice of the world?

Gratitude

What am I thankful for that will allow me to experience Beauty in my life today?

1.
2.
3.

Awareness of Connection

	Low									High
	1	2	3	4	5	6	7	8	9	10
To Self:										
To Purpose:										
To Mystery/Beauty:										

April 17

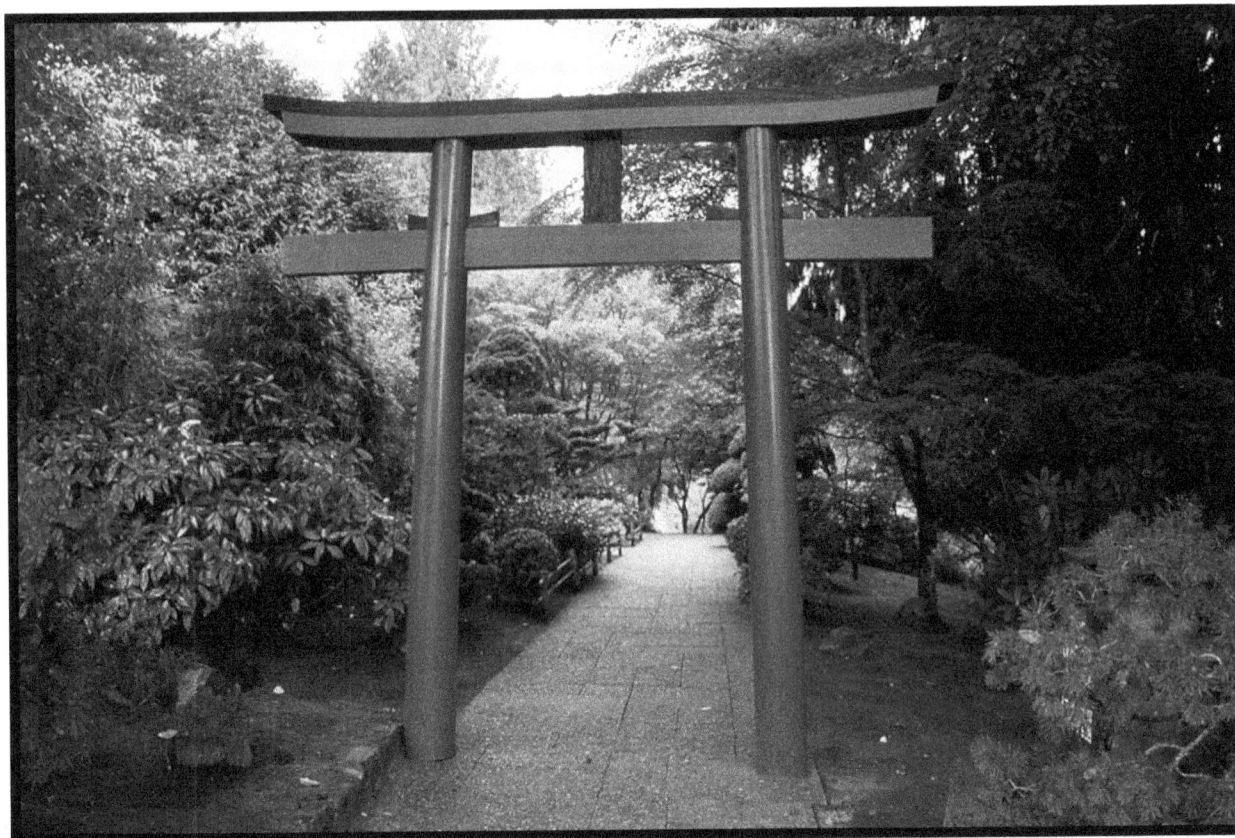

An hour was spent in silence today. This is my habit on Sunday at Quaker meeting. This was spring silence: slowing down so there is a pause between each out breath and in breath, waiting for silence to open a door, letting impatience fall to the floor and lie there unattended.

After the hour in silence a man who has been recovering from a car accident for over a year spoke. He is a large six foot, heavy framed man. He is just now able to walk without a cane. For months he has had to let people do the simplest things for him in order for his body to function. He has eaten the ashes of impatience.

It is difficult to allow the pages of the book of demands we carry to loosen from our hands for even an hour. As he limped to the car by me after our time in silence his joy was palpable, his pages not folded and stuffed into a back pocket.

Reflections:

Further Reflection

Can I use silence, my breath, to let go and be my life?

Gratitude

What am I thankful for that will allow me to experience Beauty in my life today?
1.
2.
3.

Awareness of Connection

	Low									High
	1	2	3	4	5	6	7	8	9	10
To Self:										
To Purpose:										
To Mystery/Beauty:										

April 18

Sometimes we go into a store, and it has a little gated turnstile that turns as we walk in, but only turns one way. This is the way it is with the defenses we build to keep us safe. Once they become outmoded we are trapped inside them, and the turnstile to get beyond them does not turn in the direction to get out.

Instead, we have to go to another part of the store where we have to pass through a check-out line in order to leave. Whatever baggage we picked up in the store, whatever childhood defenses we learned, we have to pay for them to get out. By that time, of course, we do not even want the old defenses: need to control, or the persona that keeps people at a distance, but still we have got to pay for these defenses before we can leave.

The tender is like the dollar bill. On one side there is a picture of a wise president, a representation of worldly wisdom. We have to pay in the tender of seeing clearly how we were benefited by the defenses, how they served us and why we now need to give them up.

On the other side of the dollar is the symbol of the pyramid with the eye in it. Payment of greater consciousness is also needed to get out of the store. The esoteric payment that is required means moving through a spiritual process that allows us to see the wounds that caused the needed defenses as gifts. This payment is harder. But of course what is hardest, once we are out of the store, is to decide that what has been dearly purchased must be left behind. The gifts come, once the price of consciousness has been paid, by leaving the old defenses right there on the sidewalk and, no longer burdened, walking into the bright and gleaming spring day. In this action, there is the awful, terrible possibility of freedom.

Reflections:

Further Reflection

Before the sun, the darkness; before the darkness a forgetting – am I ready to leave the store of attachment?

Gratitude

What am I thankful for that will allow me to experience Beauty in my life today?

1.
2.
3.

Awareness of Connection

	Low									High
	1	2	3	4	5	6	7	8	9	10
To Self:										
To Purpose:										
To Mystery/Beauty:										

April 19

Sometimes I want what seems impossible even in spring.

Reflections:

Further Reflection

Do I allow myself to experience my longing?

Gratitude

What am I thankful for that will allow me to experience Beauty in my life today?
1.
2.
3.

Awareness of Connection

	Low									High
	1	2	3	4	5	6	7	8	9	10
To Self:										
To Purpose:										
To Mystery/Beauty:										

April 20

I am told, and I tell people, that to be happy they need to learn to trust other people, to bring other people into their lives. Yet these others, who are so essential to good mental health and to the endeavors in life that bring joy, are for the most part unreliable. I am the kind of person who puts a premium on loyalty. I expect my trust to be repaid in the manner that I make my trust available to others. In doing so, I put myself up against an impossibility. Up against a denial of another's freedom.

We all must solve this conundrum on a daily basis. The only solution I know of is to take this me that is going to benefit from being connected with others and allow it to get the benefits, but not the hurts, of these connections. We can't totally insulate ourselves from the hurts, but we can learn to dodge the hurts, to see the hurts as a reflection of the other person's limitations and self-centeredness, just as our need to have others respond to us in a certain way is a reflection of our self-centeredness.

The humanness stuff is messy. One dodges the hurts by having a dodge muscle that one daily exercises. This muscle becomes strengthened by being centered in the perfect imperfectedness of our lives, and by spiritually connecting to what is greater. This connection to what is greater, to God, is what serves to move us beyond the trap of self.

If the little fragile ego is all there is, then human connection is never enough.

Reflections:

If there is something larger than me, can I experience it right now?

Gratitude
What am I thankful for that will allow me to experience Beauty in my life today?
1.
2.
3.

Awareness of Connection

	Low									High
	1	2	3	4	5	6	7	8	9	10

To Self:
To Purpose:
To Mystery/Beauty:

April 21

There is an interior geography and the one of place and landscape. Sometimes on a spring morning in April they meet. The wisteria has climbed to some impossible heights in an old tree and its purple white flowers in grape clusters hang in an air full of its wine fragrance. The inspiration of the natural world meets the simple joy of our own life force.

Then we are offered an opportunity to lose center. Some small sleight by one who loves us, lies on the ground inside our heads waiting to be picked up and shaped into clay, maybe even fired into pottery, so that we could keep it in some cabinet for the rest of our lives.

This wisteria morning, azaleas have broken out in their absurd flames and for once we leave the inner lump in our heads on the ground. Instead we go outside and plant tomatoes, peppers and eggplant. They will need cleansing rain and compost, as our actions are to the old sleight we refused to give life to.

Reflections:

Further Reflection

How might my inner landscape learn from the outer one?

Gratitude

What am I thankful for that will allow me to experience Beauty in my life today?
1.
2.
3.

Awareness of Connection

	Low									High
	1	2	3	4	5	6	7	8	9	10
To Self:										
To Purpose:										
To Mystery/Beauty:										

April 22

What are we to make of the fact that the last thing trying to escape from Pandora's box after plagues and famines was hope?

How is hope a pestilence? How is one optimistic but not hopeful? How is one open to life but not crushed by it? Giving up hope is a form of surrender. How is giving up hope a cure for our lives? Maybe giving up hope (this surrender) is about giving up willful (ego-driven) self reliance. Giving up hope is a letting go in the same way that we give up happiness in order to achieve it. Happiness is not something we achieve, rather happiness is a byproduct of living an authentically meaningful life.

Maybe giving up hope (this surrender) is about accepting life on life's terms, not fearing life's woes, but also not living in delusion about them.

Maybe giving up hope (this surrender) is about giving up on one's limited human power and knowledge and relying on the power of others, on the power of nature and on the power of the sacred, wherever and however the sacred is manifest in the world.

Maybe giving up hope (surrender) is about accepting our human frailty and that of others, but knowing that frailty is where the light, and hope that is cleaned of its willfulness curse, gets in.

Reflections:

Further Reflection

Before the clinched fist comes the clinched mind. What do I need to give up?

Gratitude

What am I thankful for that will allow me to experience Beauty in my life today?

1.
2.
3.

Awareness of Connection

	Low									High
	1	2	3	4	5	6	7	8	9	10

To Self:

To Purpose:

To Mystery/Beauty:

April 23

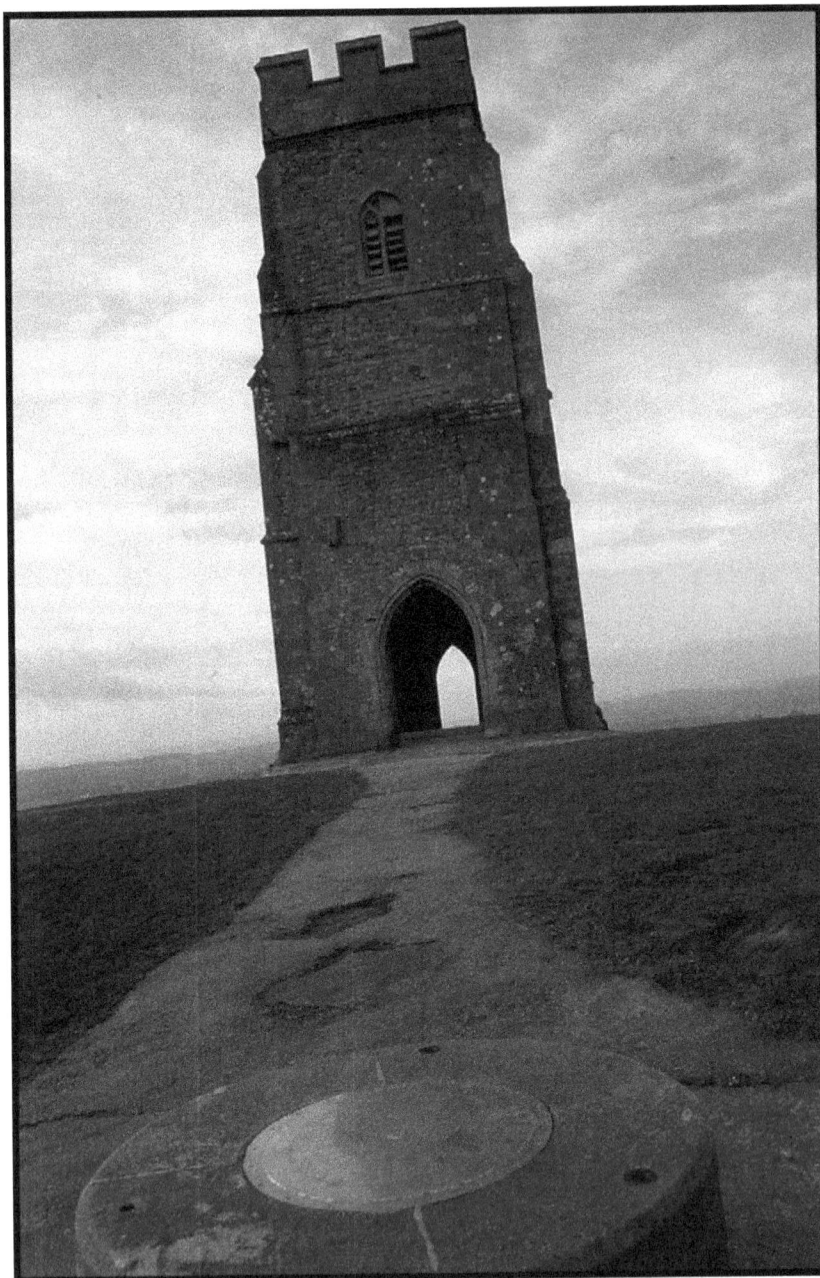

My friend said, you know there is really not that much difference between spiritual detachment and just "not giving a damn."

The point is well-made, but it focuses the issue of detachment on polarities rather than the larger more complicated issue of passion without attachment to outcome.

Longing is part of our life force. We don't want to be detached from it. But we do need detachment from the many things our ego attaches this life force to. Giving up attachment to objects of longing is like giving up hope.

We hope too much if we are alone. We are too hopeful if our hopes prevent us from seeing reality and possibility.

How do we embrace uncaring, giving up hope and aloneness and find love and possibility and the community that make these possible?

There are at least three ways that we get love, possibility and community. The imperfection in each of the ways is what sustains the longing to get there:

- The way of God – devotion to a loving, caring deity.
- The way of service –escaping the neediness of self through service.
- The way of creativity – making Beauty through creativity – making meaning greater than and larger than oneself, the making of which connects us to something larger.

Reflections:

					Further Reflection					

What is my natural path for moving beyond self to love and Beauty?

Gratitude
What am I thankful for that will allow me to experience Beauty in my life today?
1.
2.
3.

Awareness of Connection

	Low									High
	1	2	3	4	5	6	7	8	9	10
To Self:										
To Purpose:										
To Mystery/Beauty:										

April 24

What we know of human psychology is that as we grow up we construct a personality with defenses to keep us from feeling unsafe. These defenses can be to protect us from cultural harm, such as prejudices, or to protect us from family harm. The defenses are developmentally very important. They allow us to survive.

The deeper the wounding that caused the protective mechanism to form, the harder the defense is leave behind when its use has been outgrown.

I recently had dinner with a friend who has the protective mechanism of judgementalism and negativity. With these characteristics, he never needs to take responsibility for creating joy in his life, for being vulnerable to his own suffering. If there is always something out there to complain about, he remains impotent and does nothing to bring his own light into the world. His defense mechanisms have kept him stopped at the gate of life.

Reflections:

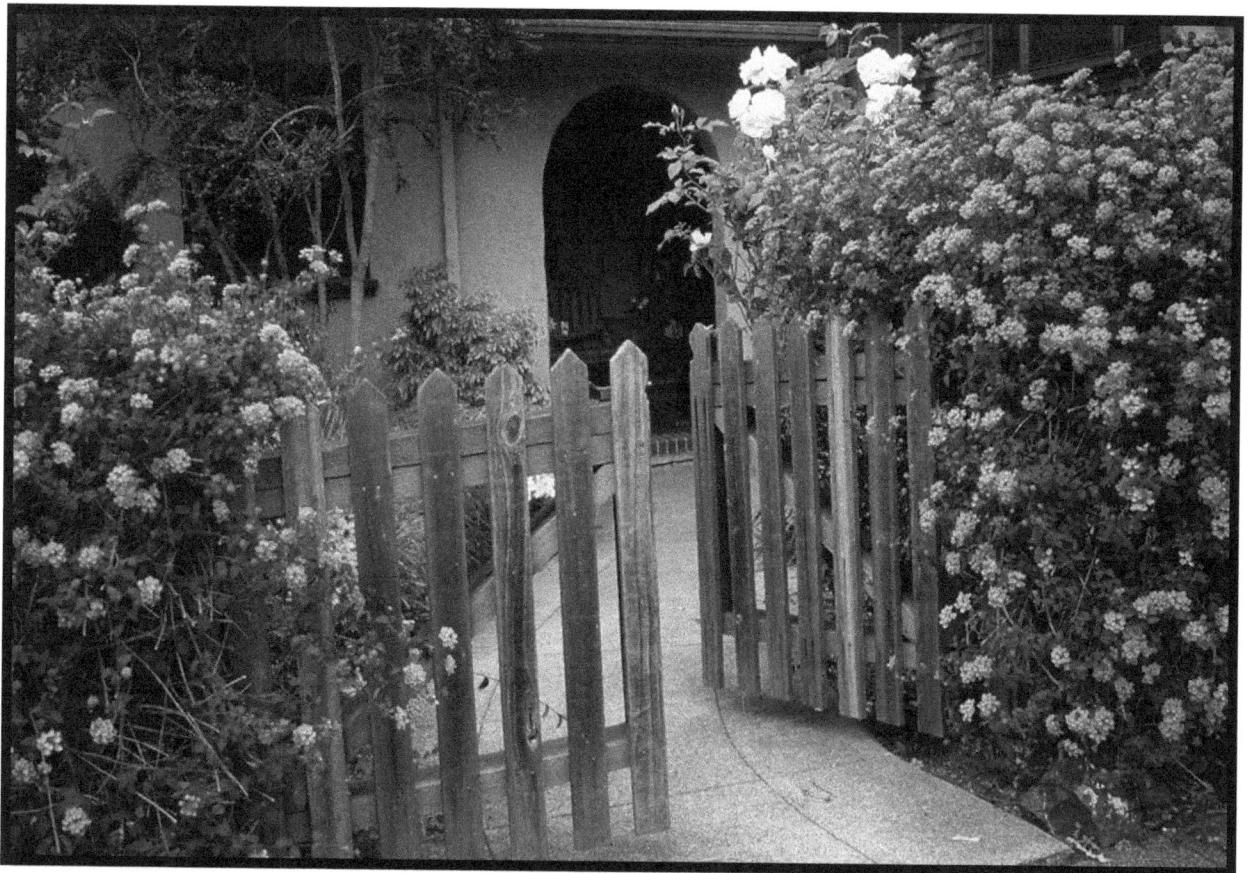

Further Reflection

Am I stuck at the gate of my life or have I walked past my protective defenses into my life?

Gratitude

What am I thankful for that will allow me to experience Beauty in my life today?

1.
2.
3.

Awareness of Connection

	Low									High
	1	2	3	4	5	6	7	8	9	10
To Self:										
To Purpose:										
To Mystery/Beauty:										

April 25

Today is the aftermath of a late cold snap. It snowed in the mountains, and the flowers, buds and newly planted tomatoes barely escaped frost.

No matter how diverse peoples' backgrounds or what one's work or purpose, weather talk is our true common language. A little quirky pressure front, like the one just now, may get neighbors talking that have not talked for weeks.

We no longer have a common religion, or civil politics, or universally celebrated cultural events to pull us together – to participate in and talk about. All we have left, maybe all we ever had, is the weather. How grateful we can be for weather's variety and occasional bluster, its predictability and its unpredictability.

The weather gives us all access to a unifying human topic, and ultimately it may be the constancy of this topic that provides a conversational presence. In all its varied forms, presence is all the help we ever need.

Reflections:

Further Reflection

How can I make the weather topic a way to more deeply interact with those around me?

Gratitude

What am I thankful for that will allow me to experience Beauty in my life today?
1.
2.
3.

Awareness of Connection

	Low									High
	1	2	3	4	5	6	7	8	9	10
To Self:										
To Purpose:										
To Mystery/Beauty:										

April 26

Today I awoke sad. Like a small terrier dog, undefined sadness has followed me all day. I have tried once or twice to peek over my shoulder. I am not sure – it is either sadness, because I am leaving on a trip and leaving my beloved behind, or it is sadness as the aftermath of all the rushing to leave. The letdown that naturally follows the build-up to a beginning.

I have always loved the rumble and rattle, the tension in the air as the plane pitches forward down the runway on take off. This sadness is like that joy. I have never known if that runaway happy expectancy is about my discontent with my normal place and being, or anticipatory excitement about what is to come. Or both. Either way, like that joy, this is a liminal sadness – being in a space between me and someone I love, between two continents, between two hemispheres. It is awareness that I want to be home. To be where the interior landscape and the outer world – the longing and what is longed for and what is – meet.

Reflections:

<u>Further Reflection</u>
Am I able to stay with my emotions, even those that occur in a liminal space?

<u>Gratitude</u>
What am I thankful for that will allow me to experience Beauty in my life today?
1.
2.
3.

<u>Awareness of Connection</u>

	Low									High
	1	2	3	4	5	6	7	8	9	10
To Self:										
To Purpose:										
To Mystery/Beauty:										

April 27

Sometimes we miss a day in our lives, and we are not sure where it was or what happened.

<u>Reflections</u>:

Further Reflection
In the rapid blur of life, what most helps me stay conscious?

Gratitude
What am I thankful for that will allow me to experience Beauty in my life today?
1.
2.
3.

Awareness of Connection

	Low									High	
	1	2	3	4	5	6	7	8	9	10	
To Self:											
To Purpose:											
To Mystery/Beauty:											

April 28

Trust grows when we have friends with whom we feel completely safe. There is a deep reassurance in feeling safe with someone, of being at home with someone. Nothing to prove. Nothing to lose. This is the sultry rain forest way of life – high humidity, a closeness that allows us to freely banter with a loved one in a way that causes no harm. The language used is like fishing with barbless hooks. It must be done skillfully and because we are able to kid harmlessly it allows intimacy to grow.

When the outer landscape meets with the inner territory of friendship, there is plenty of sunshine and rain. Life is abundant.

Reflections:

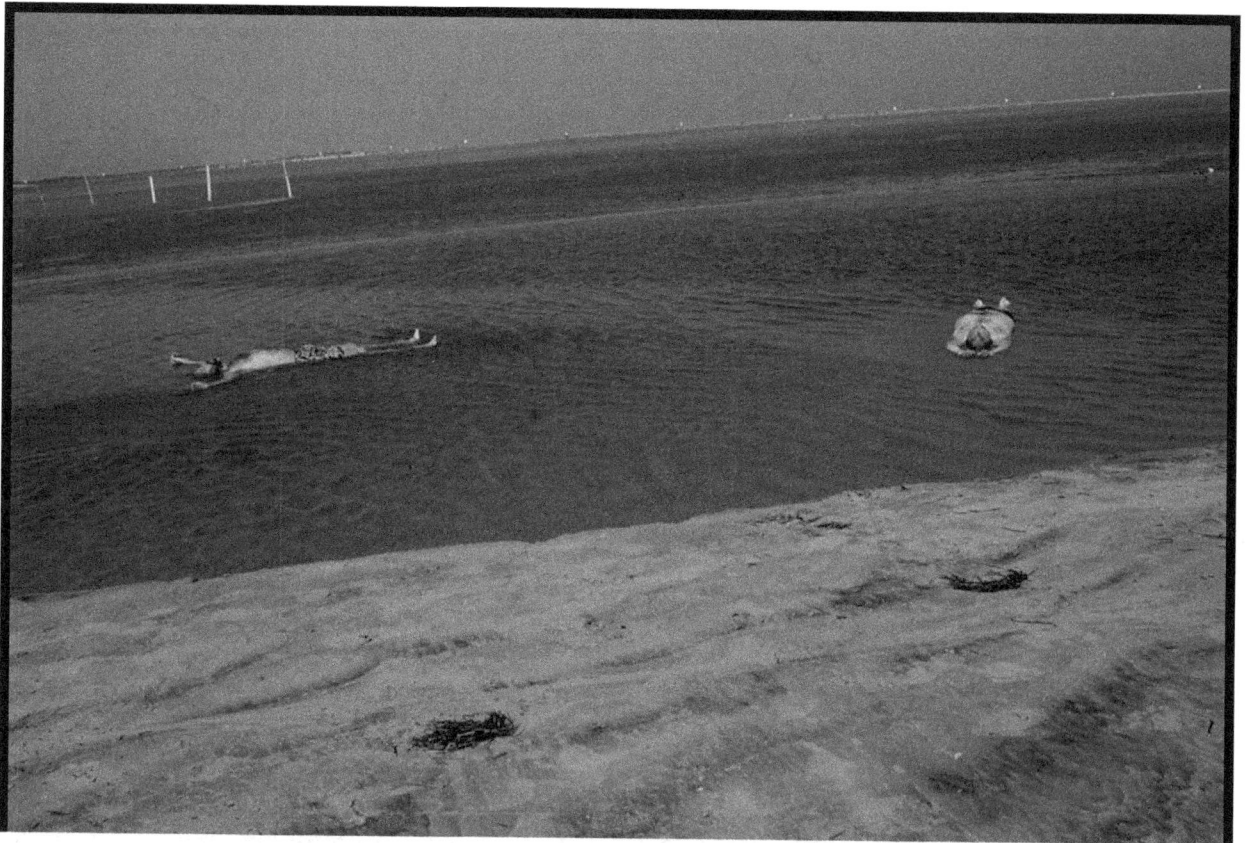

Further Reflection

What makes my relationship good in sunshine and rain?

Gratitude

What am I thankful for that will allow me to experience Beauty in my life today?

1.

2.

3.

Awareness of Connection

	Low									High
	1	2	3	4	5	6	7	8	9	10
To Self:										
To Purpose:										
To Mystery/Beauty:										

April 29

The sun is already hot, and the sand feels warm underfoot down in the Low Country. There is a special quality in the first spring days that pour heat on us. We long for it after winter, the same way we will long for a drink of cold water in the heat of this place a month or two from now. What do we learn from the first days of summer's awakening?

We learn that there is always forgiveness, that the late days of winter are about our discontent, our frustration, our attachment to a limited view. There is something so steady about the sun's heat. It is a kinesthetic blanket of forgiveness. All growth is possible from it. How often do we look inward at our own sorrow, our own plight, rather than outward at this blanket of love that assures all equally of the opportunity of life. The dolphins down in the estuary are playing close to the shore in the sun-warmed water. They seem totally convinced of abundance in their lives.

What holds us back from experiencing life's abundance is not that we are smarter than the dolphins, but that we make it more complicated. Where today can we find abundance in simplicity? Where are we needlessly hiding from the sunlight that warms everything?

Reflections:

Further Reflection

Can I let the warmth of the sun on my skin remind me that forgiveness is a part of the natural order?

Gratitude
What am I thankful for that will allow me to experience Beauty in my life today?
1.
2.
3.

Awareness of Connection

	Low									High
	1	2	3	4	5	6	7	8	9	10
To Self:										
To Purpose:										
To Mystery/Beauty:										

April 30

This morning I arose before dawn and went to the water. I walked north along the shore and the moon hung orange and ripe across the inlet and gradually slid into the treetops of an island. To the east the sky lightened and a red penumbra appeared atop the far trees until a coal of fire lay in their branches. Then the red-orange disc slowly rose like a giant balloon leaving earth for heaven.

In between, everything for miles that makes its living flying was up and out of the trees, and many with much conversation. Skimmers talking incessantly about fishing, and laughing gulls laughing as if morning depended on the seriousness of their laughter.

We cannot be long in such natural Beauty and not remember that we are a part of nature. If we really want to feel at home, that we belong, we need to be where our body feels and knows that we are naturally a part of this world. There is no better place than outside on the morning of a moon-set and a sunrise to realize we belong. And how can we make the experience of belonging a more tangible reality in our lives?

Reflections:

Further Reflection

Between the moon set and the sun rise, there is solace for the soul.

Gratitude

What am I thankful for that will allow me to experience Beauty in my life today?

1.

2.

3.

Awareness of Connection

	Low									High	
	1	2	3	4	5	6	7	8	9	10	

To Self:

To Purpose:

To Mystery/Beauty:

May 1

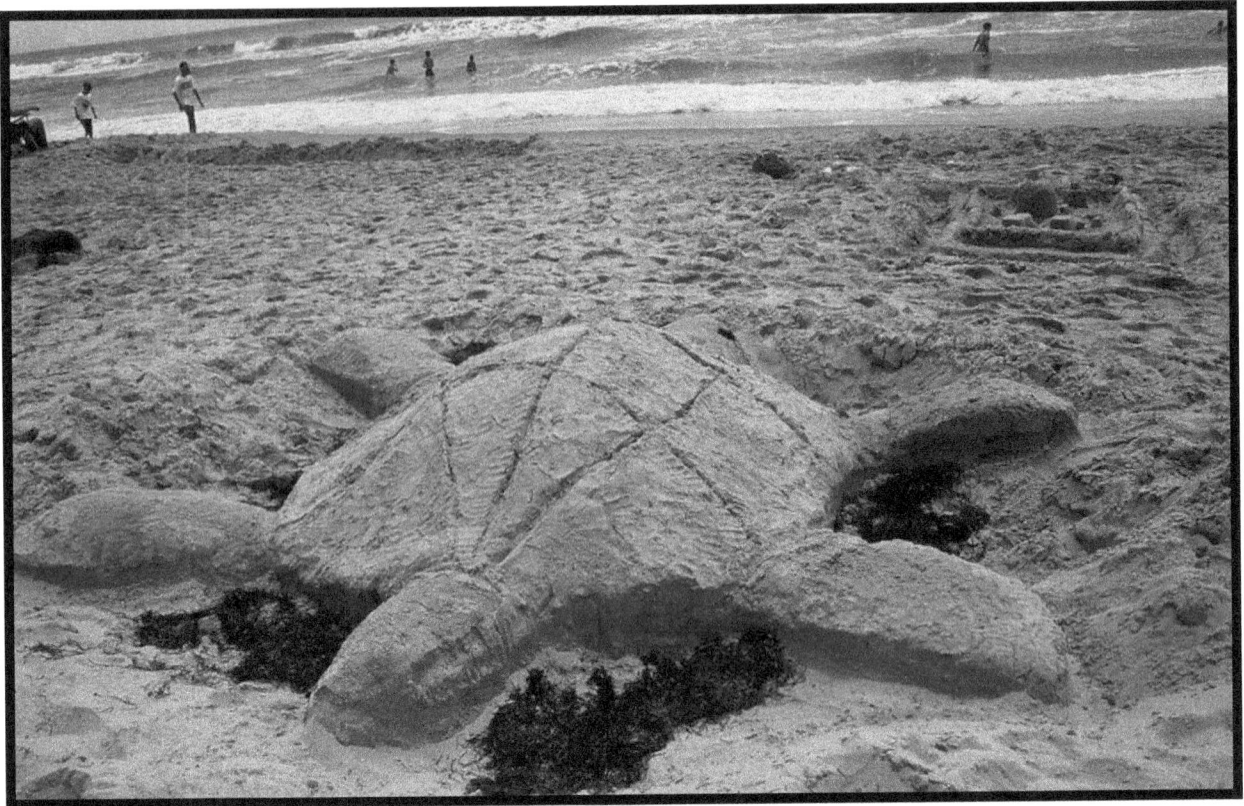

The ocean at the Great Barrier Reef is just like the human brain. Hundreds of thousands of species of coral and sea life interact through chemical messengers that protect, defend, reproduce and kill.

Coral can reproduce asexually or sexually. The sexual reproduction occurs on one day of the year along hundreds of miles of reef – the temperature is right, the chemical messengers are right and zing millions of eggs and sperms are released. They float to the top and couple up. The fertilized seeds then drop to the ocean floor to grow.

Maybe we are no different. Maybe it is just timing. We see her, like Dante saw Beatrice, and the rest is literature. Or, we pull something out of a hunk of clay and we are a potter for life. Or, we take that first loaf out of the oven, and the baker's kitchen is our eternal domain.

And maybe we are different. We grow up in the city and something pulls us all our lives to live on a farm. We never make it, what with the city wife and kids, but the farming messenger is always there in our brain. We live our lives in a place of where we are and in our longing.

We are combinations of the real and the longed for. Each shapes us. And it is the peculiar combination we each have that allows us to ask the questions we ask, to find both freedom and what is not freedom. To try to be our own god, and to long for God.

Reflections:

Further Reflection

Can I live in freedom and longing?

Gratitude

What am I thankful for that will allow me to experience Beauty in my life today?
1.
2.
3.

Awareness of Connection

	Low									High
	1	2	3	4	5	6	7	8	9	10
To Self:										
To Purpose:										
To Mystery/Beauty:										

May 2

At the aboriginal center near Cairns in Queensland, Australia, we are re-told the history of how the native population was almost completely killed off by white settlers. The Aborigines weren't even given reservations. It is impossible to say whose brand of genocide was worse, the European Americans to the North American Indians or the Spanish to the South American Indians, the Australians to the Aborigines, etc.

Ultimately, the struggle was as much cultural as racial. The Aboriginal people took totem animals and plants, and one could not destroy that plant or animal without getting permission from the totem holder. A natural stewardship was created and balance maintained.

The white man is not interested in balance, but simply exploiting what there is to be exploited, of getting and getting. As much as we are offended by the exploitation, we find it is a part of us. We see it in our impatience, in our failure to just be, rather than do. When our doing comes from a place of being, we create an internal state of balance that is reflected in the natural world.

Our treatment of native peoples asks many questions. How do we maintain an aboriginal natural-balance state of mind in a modern culture? How do we avoid cultural conflicts, where one culture feels it must destroy the other out of fear? How do we change destroying-cultures into cultures of balance, rather than just allowing them to self-perpetuate their own destiny? Is there evolutionary efficacy in compassion?

Reflections:

Further Reflection
How do I understand: "Without doing anything, let nothing be undone."

Gratitude
What am I thankful for that will allow me to experience Beauty in my life today?
1.
2.
3.

Awareness of Connection

	Low									High
	1	2	3	4	5	6	7	8	9	10

To Self:
To Purpose:
To Mystery/Beauty:

May 3

In the jungle, or I guess "rain forest" is the current politically correct term, the larger the seed, nut or fruit, the more likely it is that it will be harmful/poisonous to eat. A kind of Australian black bean for instance comes in a pod that holds three or four chestnut-like nuts. The Bama, or Aborigines as the whites call them, figured out that it took seven days of cycles of cooking and soaking to make black beans edible.

Nature's point is not puritanical. She is too luxuriant and over the top with blossoms and fruits of many sizes, hues and tastes.

No, like the poem about the Aztec painting of God hidden in a tiny pea, it is often what is small or hidden that is the source of nourishing truth. This is hard for us because we have the kind of emotional nature that prefers the burning bush experience to provide personal truth. We want the insight receptor to be hit full force by the neuro-transmitters of love, God and destiny.

Maybe this happens to some, but in the jungle of stimulation we live in, we do best looking for the small edible nuts, yearning for God in the pea, finding love in the ordinary human folly of each day.

Reflections:

Further Reflection

It is the large, colorful flower that causes all the commotion. It is the small seed that nurtures. How do I choose which one?

Gratitude

What am I thankful for that will allow me to experience Beauty in my life today?
1.
2.
3.

Awareness of Connection

	Low									High
	1	2	3	4	5	6	7	8	9	10

To Self:
To Purpose:
To Mystery/Beauty:

May 4

We either promote consciousness, or we promote unconsciousness. We do this as a culture and as individuals.

As a culture, we promote unconsciousness through spectator sports and spectator sexual imagery. The distance of the spectator is a way to deny consciousness because it creates the illusion of being separate from something. As a spectator one is caught up in the process of projection, and the process of projection induces unconsciousness.

Maybe sport is a vital community way to sublimate aggression. Maybe all the sex-based advertising is a helpful way to sublimate over-zealous sexual urges – but I doubt it. These are primary ways to stay unconscious about the power of one's own instinctual desires and avoid the challenge of making them something creative and graceful in our lives.

Some of these cultural paradigms of promoting unconsciousness apply more to men, others more to women. Yet together they promote a culture of unconsciousness. We might say evolutionary biology is controlled by women – they are the ones that choose the type of conscious, or unconscious, men with whom to mate. And in choosing, no doubt, they choose in a way to complement their own degree of consciousness.

Reflections:

Further Reflection

Where and how do I promote my unconsciousness?

Gratitude

What am I thankful for that will allow me to experience Beauty in my life today?

1.
2.
3.

Awareness of Connection

	Low									High
	1	2	3	4	5	6	7	8	9	10
To Self:										
To Purpose:										
To Mystery/Beauty:										

May 5

Today is a day to have a good time. Sometimes that is hard. The expectations around having a good time are much greater than the more limited hopes of an ordinary work day. With more limited expectations come the greater likelihood of being able to just be in the moment with what is.

Something totally new also offers this chance to be in the moment. It is amazing to see the Grand Canyon or the New York City skyline for the first time. Being in the moment, in something new, with no expectations, is an extraordinary place to be.

Particularly when we add curiosity. Curiosity comes with a sufficient sense of security that one is at home enough to take a chance – to let there be a lull in a conversation with a friend, a lull that does not have to be filled, that might move friendship deeper. Or to take a chance to speak to a stranger, or on a special occasion to say what needs to be said, to risk, to be vulnerable.

Reflections:

Further Reflection
The task of making each day special is a choice of consciousness. What do I choose today?

Gratitude
What am I thankful for that will allow me to experience Beauty in my life today?
1.
2.
3.

Awareness of Connection

	Low									High
	1	2	3	4	5	6	7	8	9	10
To Self:										
To Purpose:										
To Mystery/Beauty:										

May 6

What is it like to be connected to a non-human animal? Is there a form of consciousness that is not thinking consciousness, but non-thinking consciousness, that dwells in and grows in us and other species?

Most of what we know about ourselves, we know through our relationship to other humans. We know because of what is fed back to us in a circular loop of human interaction. Do we have this with animals? Yes, we pet owners know we do.

Do we miss it with a person of another race, or a disabled person? Maybe so. Our mirrors are not nearly as broad, as un-smudged as they might be. The dilemma then is how do we stretch the limits of what we can know and understand and at the same time stay secure enough (to do the stretching) to be reinforced in our own identity, to be ourselves?

We have to re-define ourselves as having a consciousness bigger than our identity sense. We have to expand our identity as thinkers, as feelers, as intuitors – as who we are. We have to let our consciousness grow.

Reflections:

Further Reflection

How do I limit what the world reflects back? How might I expand what the world reflects back?

Gratitude

What am I thankful for that will allow me to experience Beauty in my life today?
1.
2.
3.

Awareness of Connection

	Low									High
	1	2	3	4	5	6	7	8	9	10
To Self:										
To Purpose:										
To Mystery/Beauty:										

May 7

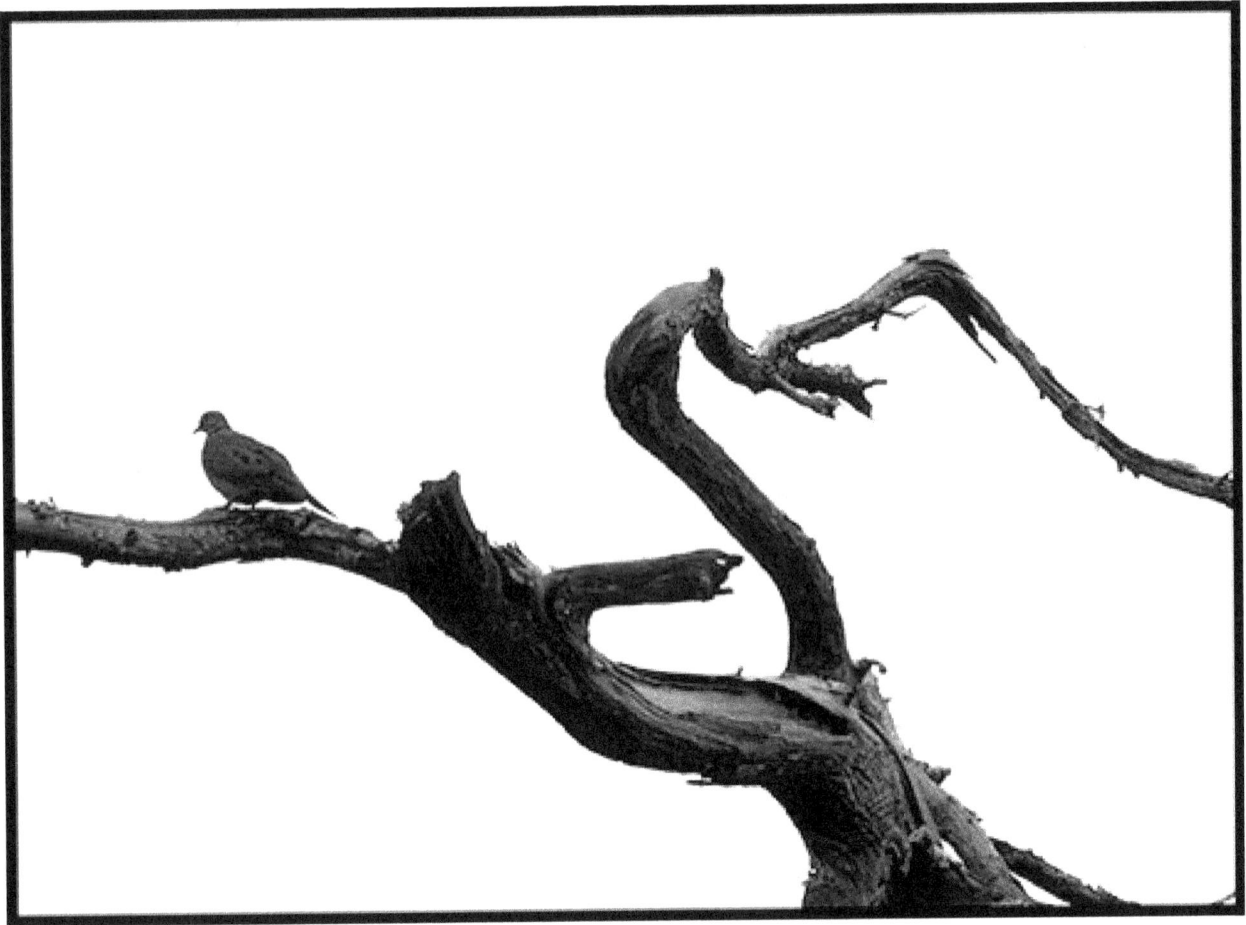

Already the hot breath of summer seems close at hand. The grass is up thick, past needing to be mowed. The garden is planted but un-mulched. There are times that it seems we can't even keep up with the natural turning of the seasons, much less email and the general haste of life.

And yet, we are most at home in our own skin when our clock is in mesh with the clock of the natural world. We sleep better when our body clock gets off daylight savings time. Food tastes better when what is prepared is what the current season has provided.

So today out of sync, feeling partially jet-lagged, there is ratitude for nature's rhythm. We are grateful to know that, of the many ways that there are to come to our lives, that one of those ways is as close as stepping out the door, sitting in the porch rocker and letting the skin of the world and our skin gently rub together.

Reflections:

Further Reflection										
How can I relax into a natural rhythm that is larger than I am?

Gratitude
What am I thankful for that will allow me to experience Beauty in my life today?
1.
2.
3.

Awareness of Connection

	Low									High
	1	2	3	4	5	6	7	8	9	10
To Self:										
To Purpose:										
To Mystery/Beauty:										

May 8

I wonder about the concept of interlocutory prayer. I have been convinced for a long time that prayer doesn't do anything to change God, but it sure does have the capacity to change the person praying.

Here is a clear and observable experiment. If we have a strong resentment against someone, pray for that person for thirty days. Before the thirty days started we would think of this person for five minutes – then various tests would be run to show the body's stress level response. After the thirty days, we would do the same tests. The experiment would show the level of stress induced by the resentment has dropped or disappeared. The subjective impression from the resenting person would be that the resentment has gone.

Could this demonstrable benefit of prayer be further increased if the prayer was offered through the assistance of one that is loved? Devotion is the great door to open the heart. Traditionally, a Roman Catholic would enlist the help of Mary; a Buddhist would enlist the aid of his or her guru or an enlightened being.

Is it possible to enlist the help of someone who has lived recently or in our lifetime? Whose help might we enlist: Black Elk, Mother Theresa, Albert Schweitzer? Or someone we know personally – our pastor or the nun at the retreat center, whose love we feel unconditionally?

This is an old-fashioned idea, but it might work to help do the heavy lifting job prayer does, which is to open the heart to this one very precious and bizarre world.

Reflections:

Further Reflection

How can I open to the possibility of experimenting with prayer?

Gratitude

What am I thankful for that will allow me to experience Beauty in my life today?

1.
2.
3.

Awareness of Connection

	Low									High
	1	2	3	4	5	6	7	8	9	10
To Self:										
To Purpose:										
To Mystery/Beauty:										

May 9

There is this Mystery of why we want what is unattainable. We see this played out in various ways in people's lives, most often on a material level. If I just had this car, this house, this boat…Or an emotional/ prestige level – if I just had this wife, or this job or my kids went to this school…

Most of the time, obtaining the object of one's desires results in wonderful euphoria, or relief, for a short while but these feelings do not last.

The hole that the objects of desire were to fill, quickly becomes empty again. This is the pursuit of false gods.

But what about spiritual longing? This is a deeper Mystery – the desire to be united with God.

This is a longing that can never be filled – an

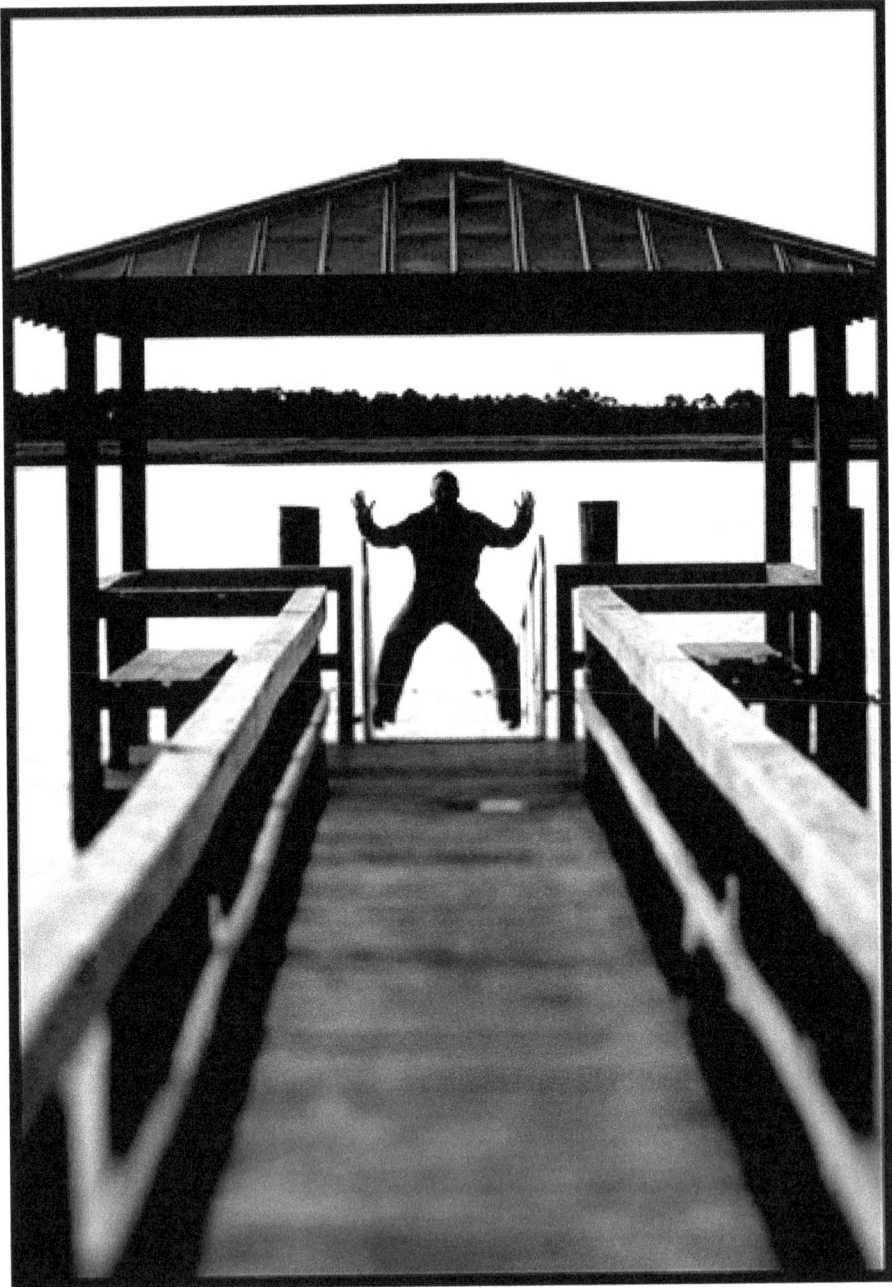

emptiness that becomes more holy as it gets bigger. It may even be the longing that all the lesser longings are vain attempts to fill.

Reflections:

What longing am I trying to fill? Or what longing am I allowing to grow?

Gratitude
What am I thankful for that will allow me to experience Beauty in my life today?
1.
2.
3.

Awareness of Connection

	Low									High
	1	2	3	4	5	6	7	8	9	10
To Self:										
To Purpose:										
To Mystery/Beauty:										

May 10

The magnolia blossom has a crisp gingery lemon smell. The magnolia tree is like a great, green scented-candle fixture, and in May it puts its lights and fragrance out. Its life is abundant; life is abundant.

As the fist-size flowers fade they lie on their green shelves like a woman's white gloves – thrown aside, slowly turning salmonish brown - gloves from a party where she danced all night with the man she loved and who loved her.

Such passages in life, that we remember in detail even years later, this tree takes in stride. Its life is a reminder that there is more abundance to be lived than we can possibly imagine.

These huge white blossoms auger the picking of blueberries – the small, quiet, perfectly round berry we pop in our mouths. Then they are gone.

Reflections:

<u>Further Reflection</u>
Where might I risk living a magnolia blossom life?

<u>Gratitude</u>
What am I thankful for that will allow me to experience Beauty in my life today?
1.
2.
3.

<u>Awareness of Connection</u>

	Low									High
	1	2	3	4	5	6	7	8	9	10
To Self:										
To Purpose:										
To Mystery/Beauty:										

A central question is how to love more than we are loved. How do we happily put out into the world more care and empathy than is given to us?

There are ways we are able to give such compassion. First, when we feel like we are continually loved in a tangible way by some source of love outside our self, then this is possible.

Secondly, when we feel like we are sufficient unto our self. When there is not some place in us that needs constant replenishing.

Thirdly, when we have a creative aspect that releases into the world its own energy, that is constantly renewed by the energy of the creativity.

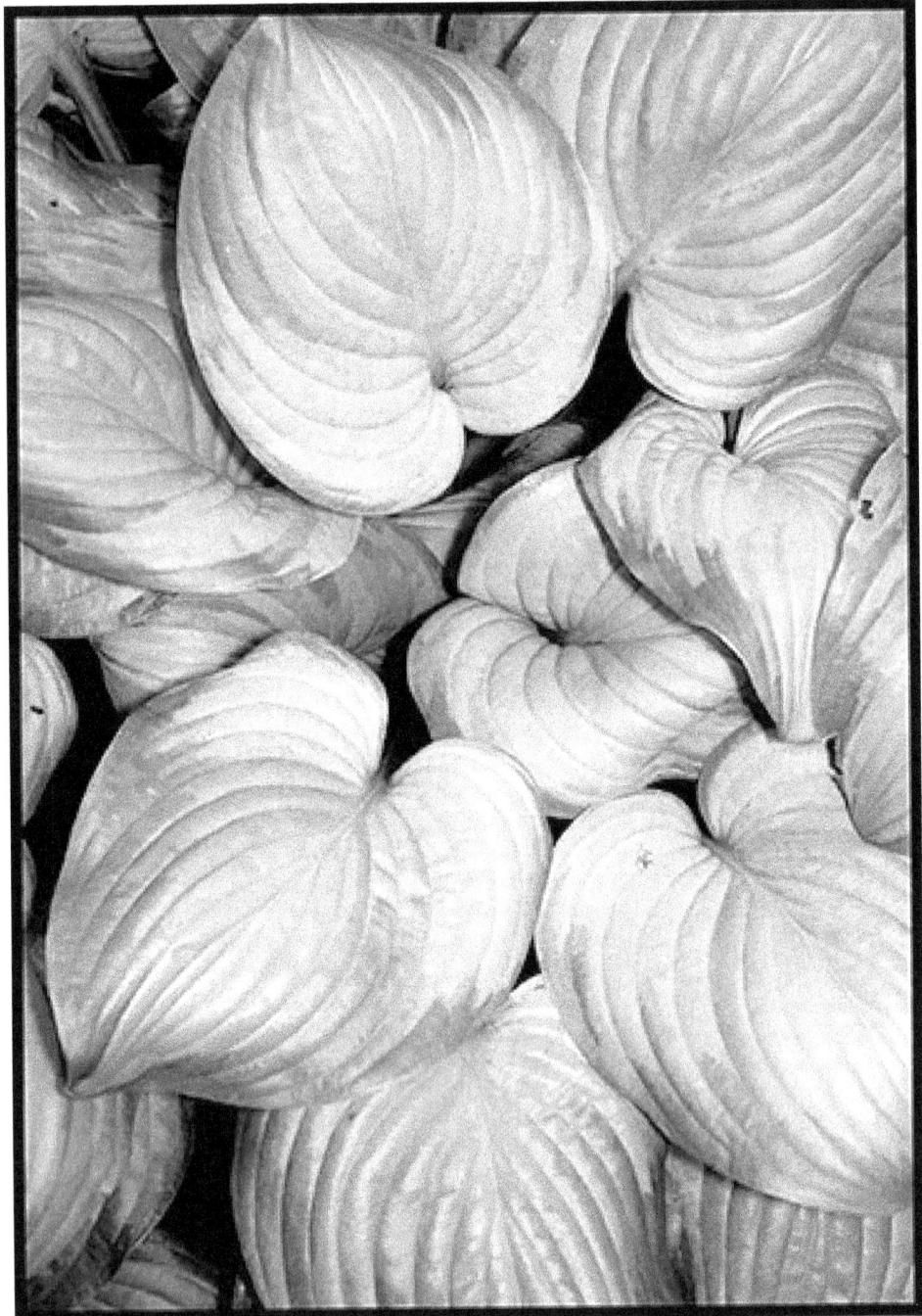

Maybe we all have aspects of these ways to compassion. We feel we are enough and can give unconditionally; our creativity alone buoys our sense of who we are; and we feel God loves us sufficiently so that we do what we would not otherwise be able to do.

Reflections:

<table>
<tr><td colspan="11" align="center"><u>Further Reflection</u></td></tr>
</table>

<u>Further Reflection</u>

How do I give to the world from a place of not needing?

<u>Gratitude</u>

What am I thankful for that will allow me to experience Beauty in my life today?

1.
2.
3.

<u>Awareness of Connection</u>

	Low									High
	1	2	3	4	5	6	7	8	9	10
To Self:										
To Purpose:										
To Mystery/Beauty:										

May 12

How do we make decisions under pressure? Sometimes in life there are those places where the road forks, and we make a choice that reverberates the rest of our lives.

Such decisions are intellectual, emotional and physical. We each put different emphasis on reasoning, emotional feelings and what is practical. But at some point we must synthesize these into meaning. What does such a decision mean? Does it mean claustrophobia? Does it mean freedom? Does it mean freedom within limits?

The last question is intriguing. What is the felt experience if we try on the decision? Do we feel free or overwhelmed or connected and challenged?

The need to feel at home is about limitation. The need to feel free is about the desire for the absence of restrictions. We all are constrained by a big container called life on this earth. Do we feel at home in this world? Do we feel graciously invited into the world that this restriction creates?

If it is all freedom, the decision likely takes we nowhere. If all constraint, the same. But it is possible to move into a container that is a place of expansion by its very limitation.

Reflections:

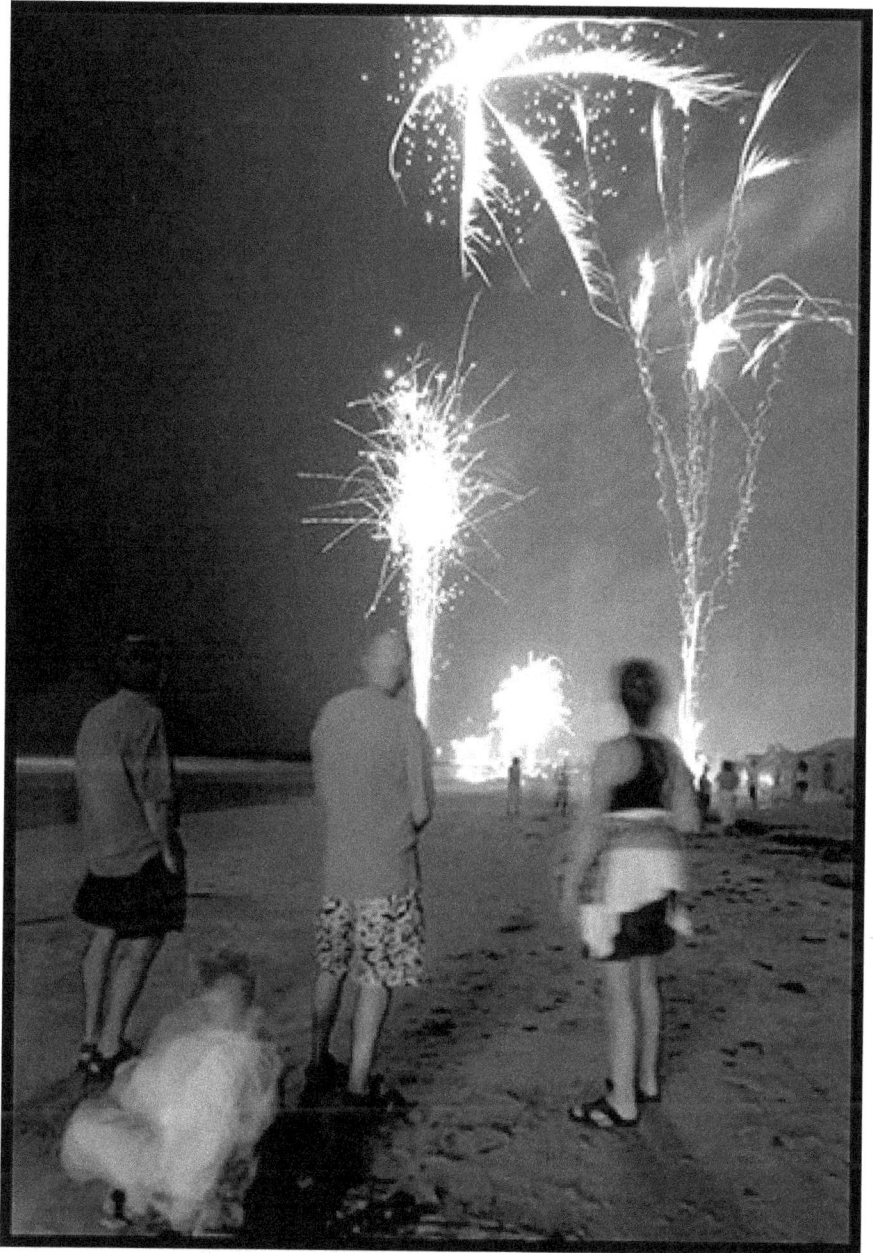

Further Reflection

Where in my life am I afraid to commit to a limitation? Am I afraid of the freedom this limitation might bring?

Gratitude

What am I thankful for that will allow me to experience Beauty in my life today?

1.
2.
3.

Awareness of Connection

	Low									High
	1	2	3	4	5	6	7	8	9	10

To Self:

To Purpose:

To Mystery/Beauty:

May 13

Today is a cool, low humidity spring morning that is like finding a perfect shell on the beach. The kind we used to find in childhood, among the multitudes of shells that have been missing at the seashore for years. It is as if another place was suddenly transported to where we are, a National Geographic Special, and we have both the frank crispness of an Australian morning, and the comfort of all our familiar southern trees and plants.

Sometimes we get that experience with someone in our lives – a morning comes when all the old defenses are for once laid aside, and the person is there complete, intact – before cancer, before old age or dementia. The air around her is cool and calm. Then the humidity settles in again, the routines of life become more prominent than the gifts of life themselves. If we are lucky, sometimes the person whom we glimpse for a moment in the cool Australian air is ourself.

Reflections:

Further Reflection										

What is the cool, crisp spring morning of myself?

Gratitude

What am I thankful for that will allow me to experience Beauty in my life today?

1.
2.
3.

Awareness of Connection

	Low									High
	1	2	3	4	5	6	7	8	9	10
To Self:										
To Purpose:										
To Mystery/Beauty:										

May 14

There is a plant in the mimosa family whose leaves curl and withdraw when touched. It is strange to have a plant respond so visibly and immediately. Yet isn't this the way we make our way through the world, prodding and poking to stimulate responses – from institutions, religions, friends and the one person we might choose, above all others, to wed.

The challenge is not about ceasing to push or probe the world around us, but about being conscious of the process of doing this. What reactions do we want from a job, a faith or a friend? Perhaps even more basic, what do we do to get the reactions we want; or what are we doing to get the reactions we don't want?

We live a life that is buffeted by reactions to our prodding. We can choose to be aware of creating a pattern that engenders the opportunities we seek in this world.

Reflections:

<u>Further Reflection</u>

Where do I push and get the reaction with which I am most happy and unhappy?

<u>Gratitude</u>

What am I thankful for that will allow me to experience Beauty in my life today?

1.
2.
3.

<u>Awareness of Connection</u>

	Low									High
	1	2	3	4	5	6	7	8	9	10
To Self:										
To Purpose:										
To Mystery/Beauty:										

May 15

My heart is very heavy. I have lost a good friend, one whom I hoped to keep for the rest of my life, one who surely would have continually enriched my life. My experience of loss is a heaviness, a weighing down.

Loss tethers us closer to the earth. Loss is about closeness to the world of matter. Matter is constantly changing, degrading, growing. My friend and I were on a growth cycle that was moving us into a higher realm. Instead, loss is moving me down to my own momentary nature here on earth, to the humility of the earth's humus.

This may be how the Pope feels when he gets off the plane and kisses the ground. I want to kiss it, to be healed by it, to let the world of unwanted change and loss dissolve the barriers of thought, expectation and desire. I want to be buried with my friend yet remain above ground – living, humble, awake.

Reflections:

Further Reflection
How can I open to the density of loss?

Gratitude
What am I thankful for that will allow me to experience Beauty in my life today?
1.
2.
3.

Awareness of Connection

	Low									High
	1	2	3	4	5	6	7	8	9	10
To Self:										
To Purpose:										
To Mystery/Beauty:										

May 16

I have always loved hibiscus. This tropical plant puts out saucer-sized flowers that each bloom for only one day. Colors are light pink, deep red, velvet white – none of the garish tones we see in new hybrids. I have a bed of deciduous hibiscus that are in full glory now. Each morning I come out and 25 to 30 blossoms are open and I am awed by the abundance of their Beauty.

They remind us how much Beauty we miss every day – sometimes it takes the bold, over-the-top to get our attention. They also remind us how much abundance there is in life. If we can just be aware of it.

These flowers throw the sensual world at us, give so much and ask nothing. They remind us that Beauty and love really do come from bottomless places. It is the limitations we place on receiving love and enjoying Beauty that can make the world, on some days, seem narrow and confined. We have all paid the price of admission; take off the guided tour headset; the banquet is spread.

Reflections:

Further Reflection
What part of the banquet am I not noticing?

Gratitude
What am I thankful for that will allow me to experience Beauty in my life today?
1.
2.
3.

Awareness of Connection

	Low									High
	1	2	3	4	5	6	7	8	9	10

To Self:
To Purpose:
To Mystery/Beauty:

The goal of mankind throughout history has been a quest for freedom. Freedom from hunger, freedom from oppression. There are multiple layers we try to cast off to be free. Just as this is true historically, it is true in our personal lives. We strive to be free of the emotional and spiritual things that seem to tie us down. Unfortunately, our efforts to be free are, from childhood and adolescence, reactions against. For many of us, we continue to be in a reactive pattern the rest of our lives. We are against this about church or that about government. We have not chosen freedom, but to be defined by our reaction against.

Similarly, at an emotional level rather than making free choices we often choose to seek the safe harbor of a coping mechanism. Whether it

is drinking, denial, projecting on others etc. – the coping mechanism becomes the prison house in which we live. We don't make free choices. We engage instead in conduct that will allow us not to feel a certain way, so that we can shut off the anxiety that goes with actually making a free decision.

Reflections:

Further Reflection

How do I limit my freedom?

Gratitude

What am I thankful for that will allow me to experience Beauty in my life today?

1.
2.
3.

Awareness of Connection

	Low									High
	1	2	3	4	5	6	7	8	9	10
To Self:										
To Purpose:										
To Mystery/Beauty:										

May 18

Freedom does not operate in a vacuum. Paradoxically, in order to be free there has to be structure. There has to be form for there to be emptiness. The clay pot is the form that holds the emptiness. To be free, we have to have a form that gives us the capacity to have courage to make choices. We have courage about things we value. We must know our values in order to know how to make decisions to put those values into effect.

What are the values that guide our lives? Where in our lives do we choose to avoid putting them into effect?

Reflections:

Further Reflection

Without a cup our lives will never runneth over. What is my cup?

Gratitude

What am I thankful for that will allow me to experience Beauty in my life today?

1.
2.
3.

Awareness of Connection

	Low									High
	1	2	3	4	5	6	7	8	9	10
To Self:										
To Purpose:										
To Mystery/Beauty:										

Rilke in his *Letters to a Young Poet* makes the often quoted remark about the importance of living the questions. We grow by living the ambiguities in our lives, not necessarily by solving them. Ultimately life is a Mystery. If we are living our lives fully, then we are living close to this core of Mystery and the only meaningful answers will be the ones that allow us to be more fully present in that Mystery.

Many of us back up from life when we get close to Mystery: the Mystery when a friend is dying; the Mystery when a parent in pain wants us to bring extra morphine; the Mystery when a child must push away from us in order to find himself.

There are many mysteries in life, but too often we find ourselves focused on coping rather than following Rilke's advice and living the Mystery. When the pain, or anxiety, of being in the Mystery becomes too much we retreat to drinking or some other addictive substance, or process or denial. The dilemma of Mystery suggests an answer to a perennial theological question: How to love God?

To love God is to live the questions. The deeper they are lived the greater the love of Mystery of God is expressed. What is the primary question life is offering us to live that pulls us more into Mystery right now?

Reflections:

Further Reflection
Where do I not seek answers but live fully the questions of my life?

Gratitude
What am I thankful for that will allow me to experience Beauty in my life today?
1.
2.
3.

Awareness of Connection

	Low									High
	1	2	3	4	5	6	7	8	9	10
To Self:										
To Purpose:										
To Mystery/Beauty:										

May 20

Sometimes we can get up too early. Sometimes whirling thoughts and feelings that won't calm down get us up at four in the morning. We get up so we can avoid these thoughts and feelings. To avoid their using our drowsiness to bounce un-tethered in and out of our conscious mind. We get up as an act of avoidance, but the thoughts and feelings are still with us. The anxiety that clings to them like honey on a spoon will not be wiped clean by simply getting up.

So what do we do? We go ahead and get a cup of tea, some caffeine from our favorite morning source. Then we sit still and reflect on what the anxiety is about. This is a mental process. Then we see if we can just sit and experience the anxiety itself. This is an emotional process. Just doing the mental process will give us insight, but actually leave us more, rather than less, neurotic. Just doing the emotional process will calm us down, but we will have learned nothing, and be in fine shape to re-experience the anxiety again once a suitable trigger comes along to initiate our wakefulness at 4:00 a.m.

Our dreams are our organic process for working out unconscious material. But if this material is waking us, we can get up too early and avoid, or we can get up and resolve the issue. Sitting with the emotion is the hardest part. There is a fear that it won't go away, or it will overwhelm. But it is just energy, e-motion. If we give it attentive space, it will work itself out and naturally dissipate. Focus on where it is in the body. Let the mind feed it with thoughts and we are putting wood on the fire. Just watch it and the fire will die and the embers cool.

Reflections:

Further Reflection
Do I have the kind of arrogance that allows me to think I can solve an emotional issue with a mental process?

Gratitude
What am I thankful for that will allow me to experience Beauty in my life today?
1.
2.
3.

Awareness of Connection

	Low									High
	1	2	3	4	5	6	7	8	9	10
To Self:										
To Purpose:										
To Mystery/Beauty:										

May 21

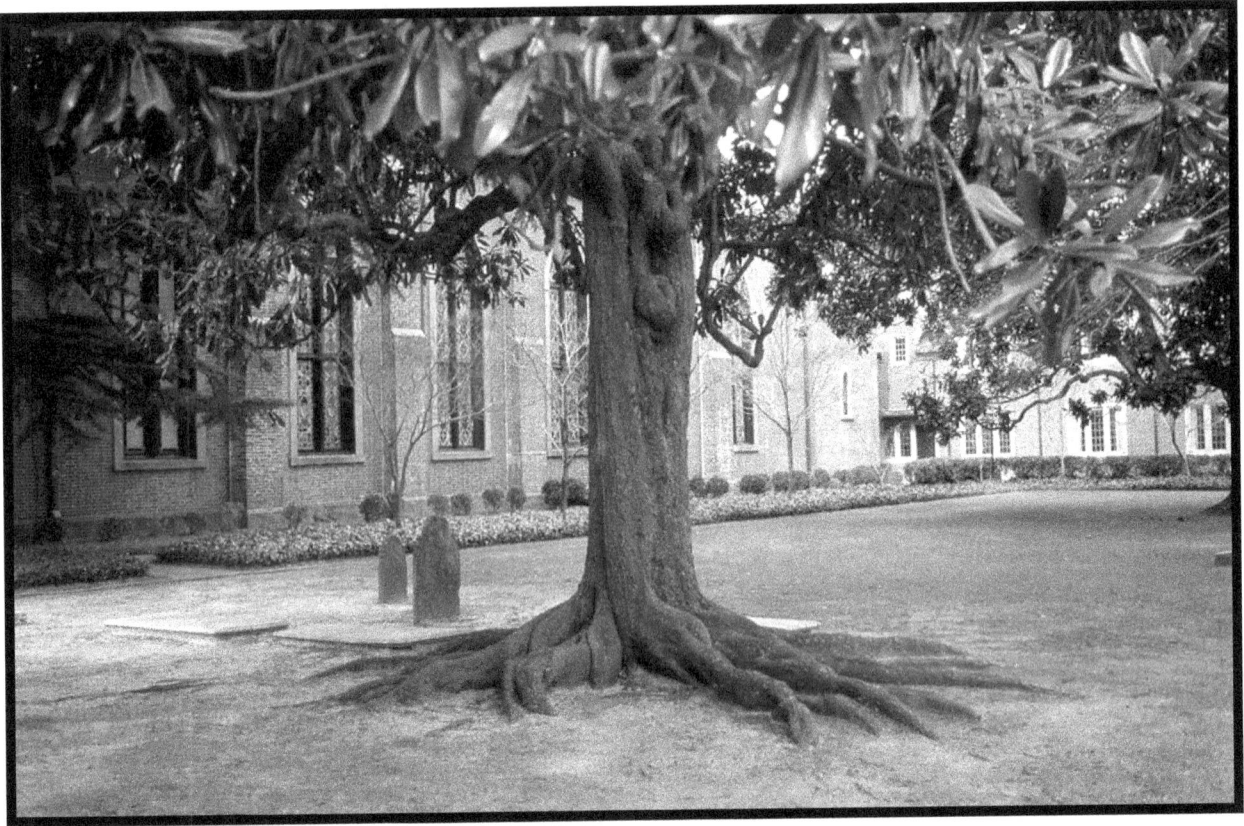

God is the question. God is the answer. What question we might well ask? Whatever the biggest question is, the largest Mystery, that we can hold. Hopefully, as our lives grow, we are asking bigger and bigger questions. Or, smaller and smaller ones. For we see ultimate meaning occurs always in the land of paradox. Each morning as we arise we are at a new beginning and we are at a conclusion. The beginning and the ending are the same point. Where we are seeking to go, we are already.

If we are half way through our life and it is not beginning to be more and more full of paradoxes, we are likely going the wrong way. If an area of our life seems full of paradox, this is a clue that we are living that area fully. For example, if we love the church and the deep gifts it brings us – connection to others and to a Power beyond ourselves – and at the same time we hate the shallowness and hypocrisy that can go on in a religious institution, yet we have become comfortable with this paradox, then we are beginning to live fully and truthfully in that place.

In this way, the central Mystery about life is God, and the answer to that Mystery is God. Intellectually these are just foolish word games; paradox is real only when it is lived in and experienced.

Reflections:

Further Reflection
Where do I live paradox in my life?

Gratitude
What am I thankful for that will allow me to experience Beauty in my life today?
1.
2.
3.

Awareness of Connection

	Low									High
	1	2	3	4	5	6	7	8	9	10
To Self:										
To Purpose:										
To Mystery/Beauty:										

May 22

Meaning by its nature has to be embodied to be real. In our heads, two conflicting ideas exist only in antagonism. But life itself, and the Mystery that holds life, is larger than that duality.

If we are living open lives not forced to conform to some preconceived idea of who we are, then we are likely living in paradox. We can live out ideas that seem to conflict and be living into a larger truth, rather than just the conflicting ideas.

What paradoxes do we live in? Are we at home in some larger truth of paradox, or does being there represent unresolved conflicts within us?

<u>Reflections</u>:

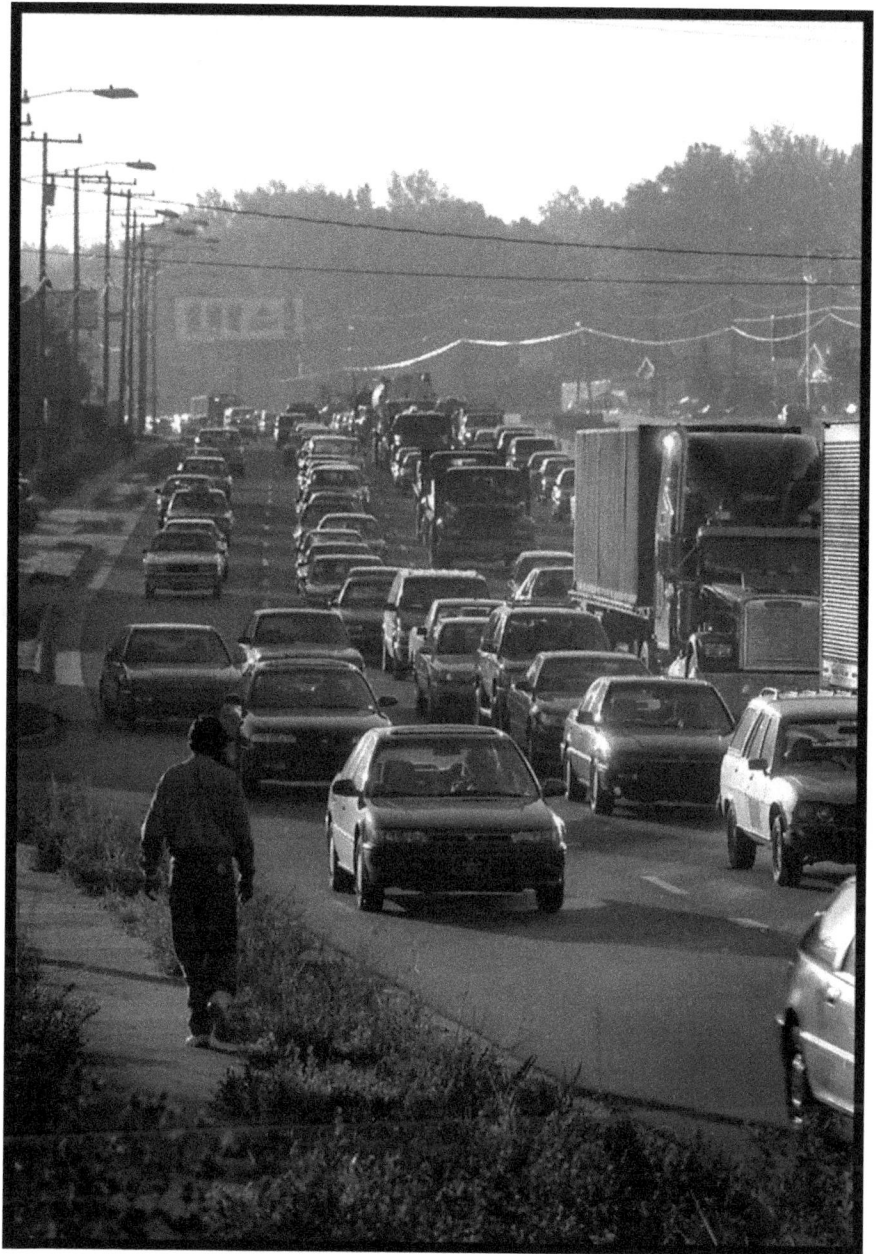

<u>Further Reflection</u>
Birth and death are paradoxes, so is everything else in between. Where do I live in paradox?

<u>Gratitude</u>
What am I thankful for that will allow me to experience Beauty in my life today?
1.
2.
3.

<u>Awareness of Connection</u>

	Low									High
	1	2	3	4	5	6	7	8	9	10
To Self:										
To Purpose:										
To Mystery/Beauty:										

May 23

This morning a slow rain soaks the Low Country after a long period of dryness. Yesterday, I noticed that resurrection fern along the tops of the large limbs and trunks of live oak trees was brown and dried up. Live oaks are the deep South trees whose outer branches are often draped in Spanish moss creating an instant Faulkner stage set. Like Spanish moss, though of less fame, the resurrection fern is not parasitic but simply grows in the rough furrows of the live oak tree's bark.

Later today, after this rain, the resurrection fern will come back from the dead and send up green shoots of promise and possibility. What if we lived in the arms of a huge tree of Grace and strength? What if we could access some new water of life and break out of the browns and grays of our lives into a fresh green vibrancy? The resurrection fern does not hesitate, once the rains come, to become more of what it is. What about us? What is the new water we desire in our lives? And what do we wish to create with it?

Reflections:

Further Reflection

What do we wish to grow anew in our lives?

Gratitude

What am I thankful for that will allow me to experience Beauty in my life today?
1.
2.
3.

Awareness of Connection

	Low									High
	1	2	3	4	5	6	7	8	9	10
To Self:										
To Purpose:										
To Mystery/Beauty:										

May 24

Each day is a choice. We can move toward being more consciously who we are in this world, in a dance in which we let our best be the edge that meets the place of greatest possibility in the world. Or, we can avoid the self knowledge of what we are and who we might truly become.

Even if we embrace the discovery of self knowledge, our fear can still cause us to avoid an encounter with the world with its heartache and uncertainty. Even when we have self knowledge and do not fear the world's uncertainty, it is likely that not much will flower without safety and love. The live oak tree that holds resurrection fern along its boughs that comes back to life is a good symbol of this holding. Another image of harmony and safety is experienced by taking the time to listen to the soft rain, melting us and this world into a new creation.

Reflections:

Further Reflection

Where in my life am I most receptive to making a choice of greater consciousness?

Gratitude

What am I thankful for that will allow me to experience Beauty in my life today?
1.
2.
3.

Awareness of Connection

	Low									High
	1	2	3	4	5	6	7	8	9	10
To Self:										
To Purpose:										
To Mystery/Beauty:										

I have been away at a retreat living a monastic style life for a week though not monastic in any sense of deprivation. The food has been excellent, the accommodations basic but more than adequate. No, what has been monastic has been the rhythm of life during this week, the form of the container for life. Those old monks had a few centuries during the flowering of the monastic period to get down a contemplative rhythm. No cell phones, no internet. Regardless of the order, or whether the monks were primarily making wine or cheese or copying manuscripts, their day was designed to be a perfect form for living life. The day's rhythm was designed most advantageously to create joy, creativity and wonder with life.

All art in some way deals with this same issue – what is the optimal form for the opportunity for freedom and creative expression. Most artists learn the classical forms so that they are second nature, before there is the opportunity for their own creativity and self-expression to emerge. In the East, there is the emphasis on getting the form right.

In the West, the emphasis is on freedom and self-expression. In between lies the truth: a form we must each discover which most adequately holds the greatest opportunity for our freedom, joy and Beauty.

<u>Reflections:</u>

<u>Further Reflection</u>

What is the form that holds my truth, my Beauty?

<u>Gratitude</u>

What am I thankful for that will allow me to experience Beauty in my life today?
1.
2.
3.

<u>Awareness of Connection</u>

	Low									High
	1	2	3	4	5	6	7	8	9	10
To Self:										
To Purpose:										
To Mystery/Beauty:										

May 26

The monastics developed their Rules of Life to define a form of work, study, play, and worship that was most conducive to the flowering of the human spirit. They had plenty of time to tinker with the pattern to try to find what might work best. We would do well to heed the underlying notion that there is a pattern for each of us that is most conducive to leading full and joyful lives.

We have a choice. We can blindly let the technologies and demands of others and the marketing of our culture define the pattern we live, or we can consciously define one for ourselves. In other words, we can be servants of some other agenda, or we can consciously take responsibility to define our own. A retreat is a good way to start figuring out what is best for us. Developing a form for our lives is not just an intellectual task of figuring out what sounds good. Rather it is helpful to live in a routine different from our norm, to get a bodily sense of where we might be called to live most vibrantly.

Are we willing to take time out and explore life patterns, seeking the right pattern to nurture the flow of our lives?

Reflections:

Further Reflection

We cannot create happiness in our lives/ we can only change the patterns in our lives that create the possibilities of the kind of lives we want.

Gratitude

What am I thankful for that will allow me to experience Beauty in my life today?

1.
2.
3.

Awareness of Connection

	Low									High
	1	2	3	4	5	6	7	8	9	10
To Self:										
To Purpose:										
To Mystery/Beauty:										

May 27

Life is developmental. We know this instinctively from a biological perspective. We all experience in our families, or the families of others, the process of watching children develop physically. We see there are times when the young child is more focused on learning fine motor coordination, other times when learning language is center stage. The biology of development from infant to child to adolescent to young adult to mature adulthood is clear and logical. We now know that the human brain does not actually complete its development until our early twenties.

What is less visible, but just as real, is our psychological and spiritual development. This development encompasses our whole life and, like our biological development, goes through a series of stages. I am writing this, and you are reading this, because, regardless of age, we have reached that point in life where we need to move on beyond limiting emotional beliefs and psychological defenses. We wish to live a more vibrant, free and joyous life – that is, we wish to expand the spiritual dimensions of our lives.

The starting point to move further along our developmental path is to know where we are. The great barrier to this insight is our desire not to experience where we are stuck. Our desire to avoid leads down two paths: over and under. We may seek to avoid experiencing where we are by seeking to transcend, by becoming spiritual. Sometimes we recognize a desire to be spiritual as a desire to escape and sometimes we don't.

When we don't, we may end up, for example, going to India to live in an ashram for a few years until we are ready to come home and face the pain of having grown up in an alcoholic family. The second path is that instead of going up to avoid we go down. We go more into matter. We become addicted to alcohol, sex, relationships, work or anything that will give us short fleeting feelings of escape from what we are avoiding.

After we realistically assess where we are, we need to know where we are going. Often we know the general direction. Sometimes we are lucky and see clearly the next place we wish to be.

Once we know where we are and where we want to go, then what we need is a map of the way to get there and a guide to help find the route. A spiritual map is a set of practices that is going to move us toward our goal. Our guide is someone who has already followed the road ahead of us, at least as far as the next rest stop.

Spiritual growth can be scary. We are asked to move out of our comfort zones. This is extremely hard to do without a good map, a guide and the fellowship of others along the same path.

Reflections:

Further Reflection
Do I clearly perceive where I am along the path of emotional and spiritual growth?

Gratitude
What am I thankful for that will allow me to experience Beauty in my life today?
1.
2.
3.

Awareness of Connection

	Low									High
	1	2	3	4	5	6	7	8	9	10
To Self:										
To Purpose:										
To Mystery/Beauty:										

May 28

The developmental stages of emotional and spiritual change are fluid. Things happen to us, we encounter new responsibilities and new circumstances. When this occurs we enter a liminal process that is always less secure – we move from a felt sense of who we are to a more uncertain sense of not being sure who we are and what our purpose is. These liminal spaces are the times when the turtle is without a shell, or the snake is without a skin. By shedding the too-small shell, or the old skin, we are able to grow into a new, roomier shell, or a larger skin. But in the time of change we are more vulnerable, more emotionally and spiritually exposed.

We stay stuck in liminal space when we are caught in an addiction that we cannot break, or we go to India and cannot leave the guru.

Our liminal space experiences are often experienced as crises. Often there is a strong pull in different directions. Our spiritual journey is to live into these tensions. We live into them not to figure out how to make it all work "correctly," but until living into them allows these tensions to resolve themselves in some paradoxical way.

Our spiritual growth occurs by living into the liminal spaces of our lives and allowing those spaces and who we are to interact and become something new. We become vegetarians who eat meat at certain times. Or, devout church-goers who occasionally go fishing on Sunday. Or, pacifists who love martial arts. These resolutions are never intellectually solved problems. Always what is needed for us to be free to grow in the vulnerable place of liminal space is the acceptance and love of those near us. This becomes the container that sustains us when our psychic container is being shed as we go through the process of building a new one. Because human acceptance and love is always imperfect, often it is the emotional tie between oneself and a loving, caring God that makes the transition possible.

Reflections:

Further Reflection

Where might I need support and care to allow myself to experience a place of change in my life?

Gratitude

What am I thankful for that will allow me to experience Beauty in my life today?

1.
2.
3.

Awareness of Connection

	Low									High
	1	2	3	4	5	6	7	8	9	10

To Self:

To Purpose:

To Mystery/Beauty:

The developmental stages of maturing revolve around how we are in relation to self and others. As a young adult we are pulled by two tensions: to explore intimacy with another, to share work and life, and to grow and protect our sense of independence as an adult. We are pulled both toward mating and toward consolidating our recently gained sense of self-being and independence.

In our mid-adult years we feel a social pull outward. We get on boards of directors, join civic groups. At the same time there is a pull inward toward greater intimacy with a few people. This pull toward intimacy is also a pull toward greater self knowledge because it is only through our intimate connections with others that we truly get to know who we are. Because in America we are so focused on the outward expansion toward others at mid-life, we often neglect the inner pull and we have the common occurrence of a mid-life crisis. Our psyches in effect force us into a liminal space to encounter at a deeper level who we are at this stage of our lives. Sometimes the mid-life crisis is an abrupt jarring. We run off with another in a mad love affair because we have neglected intimate love in our marriage for years. We buy the new sports car because we have been working so hard we have forgotten how to play. An aspect of who we are that has been repressed, comes fighting forward with a vengeance. Like the daffodil pushing up through the snow to bloom in spring, the life force in us will not be denied.

In late adulthood, we face an understanding not only of self and life's richness and meaning, but also of the inevitability of death. In other words, just as we begin to realize that in some relative respect we have figured it out – who we are and what we do well – we are faced with the reality that it will soon be over. We have at this point in our lives the greatest hope and the greatest despair.

The spiritual task through all these developmental stages is not to repress and not to act out, but to live the tension fully so that a natural resolution will occur. Holding this tension may be experienced as suffering, but it is not gratuitous suffering. This is real soul expansion work in progress.

Reflections:

Further Reflection									
Where am I today in the developmental process of maturing? What issues are front and center at this stage of my life?									
Gratitude									
What am I thankful for that will allow me to experience Beauty in my life today?									
1.									
2.									
3.									
Awareness of Connection									
Low								High	
1	2	3	4	5	6	7	8	9	10
To Self:									
To Purpose:									
To Mystery/Beauty:									

May 30

Another way to look at the developmental stages we go through would be:

- build skills in the outer world
- learn how to use these skills both for self and others
- learn heart skills to discern who we are, acceptance of who we are and release of psychological defenses that hold us apart
- learn that our beingness, not our doingness is who we are – grow in our ability to share our beingness.

All sorts of things can come along in these four stages to give us an opportunity to be in liminal space. Birth of a child, loss of a job, death of a family member – these are triggers that can send us into a liminal space where we have to confront the meaning of the stage of life where we are and contemplate some kind of adjustment. As we get older somehow the ante gets raised and the tensions of mortality, which were well below the surface, have to be experienced in a more real or different way.

Any kind of unprocessed trauma can leave us stuck in a developmental phase. The psyche in a defensive reaction may push us to skip for many years the experience of the trauma. When this happens we can be left stuck. Such phrases as, "She had to grow up too quick." or "He never had a chance to learn to make friends." encapsulate some of these types of dilemmas.

Reflections:

<u>Further Reflection</u>

Where in my life have I tried to escape a phase of my life because it seemed too difficult?

<u>Gratitude</u>

What am I thankful for that will allow me to experience Beauty in my life today?

1.
2.
3.

<u>Awareness of Connection</u>

	Low									High
	1	2	3	4	5	6	7	8	9	10

To Self:

To Purpose:

To Mystery/Beauty:

May 31

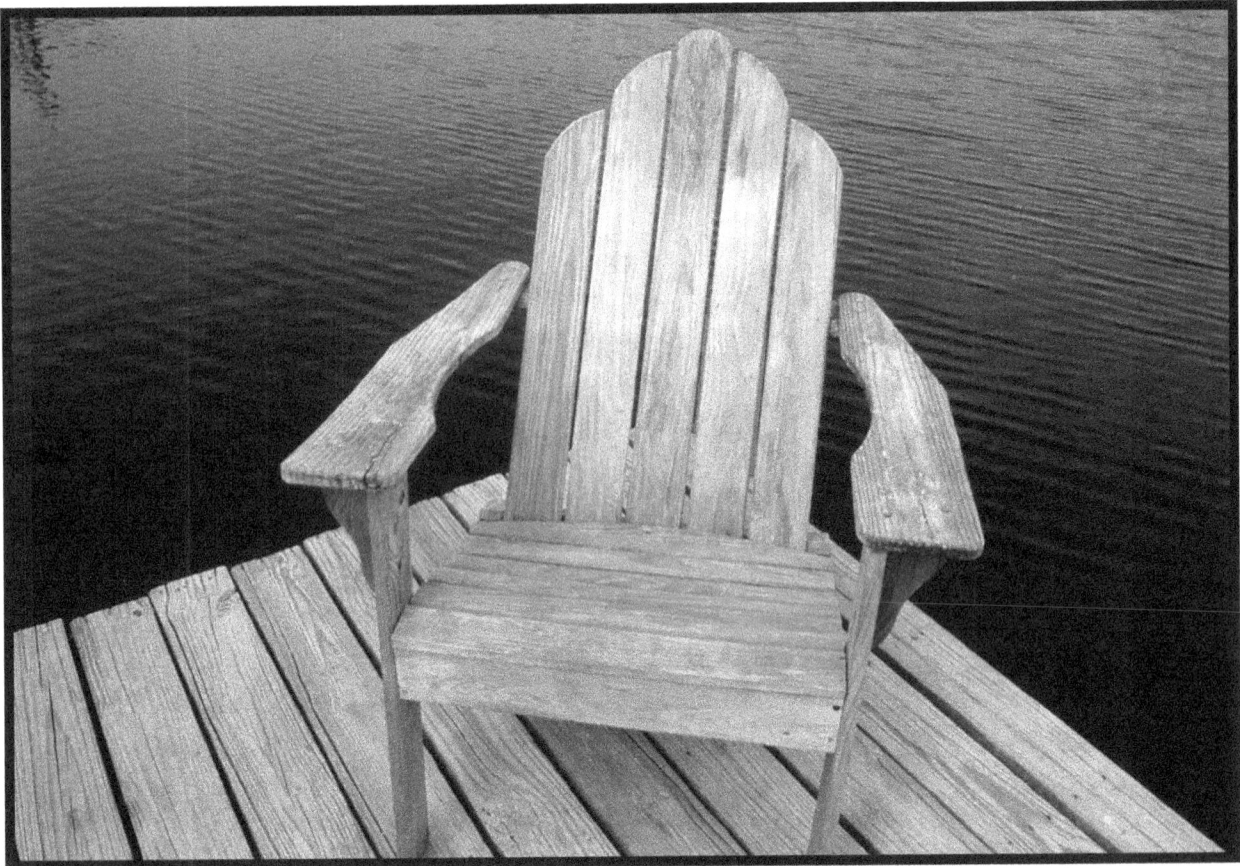

While there are spiritual solutions to life issues at any age, it is primarily in the second half of life that we come to grips with our spiritual journey. (Trauma or chronic illnesses, like alcoholism, can force us to do this at a much earlier age.)   What appears to be a call to a spiritual journey too early in life can be an effort to escape from some aspect of emotional growth caused by serious early childhood wounding. In such cases the path of avoidance may be an intense and profound experience, but the spiritual journey will be a bit circuitous.

Once we begin a spiritual journey, it is always an experiential process. There is no figuring it out in the head by analyzing and thinking. The spiritual process is by definition a lived process since it involves us bodily, mentally, emotionally and spiritually – in fact it is as a spiritual process that all of these aspects of our humanness are tied together in a coherent way.

The first step in this process is often a rejection of old ideas, or a new way of understanding the ideas that we grew up with and sustained us earlier in life.   This is appropriate and developmentally correct, for in the early years our task was to build a way to understand ourselves in the outer world. We needed to develop an ego.

For the less religiously oriented of us, the first step on the spiritual journey may be a realization that our egos – what we accomplish, what we say and do, are not sufficient to make us feel fulfilled – that there is still something missing. For those growing up in a religious tradition, it is coming to the intuitive understanding that our ideas about our religion, the religious dogma if you will, does not explain our life in a sufficient way – that there is still something missing.

In both cases, the Self, whether it is of a non-believer or a believer, realizes that the experience of the ego self is incomplete. So the spiritual journey begins when we realize that no matter what we have accomplished, how many people like us, whatever fame, power or fortune we have acquired – something is still missing. It is with the mystery of something unknown missing that the spiritual journey begins.

Reflections:

Further Reflection

Do I have everything in my life or is something missing?

Gratitude

What am I thankful for that will allow me to experience Beauty in my life today?
1.
2.
3.

Awareness of Connection

	Low									High	
	1	2	3	4	5	6	7	8	9	10	

To Self:

To Purpose:

To Mystery/Beauty:

June 1

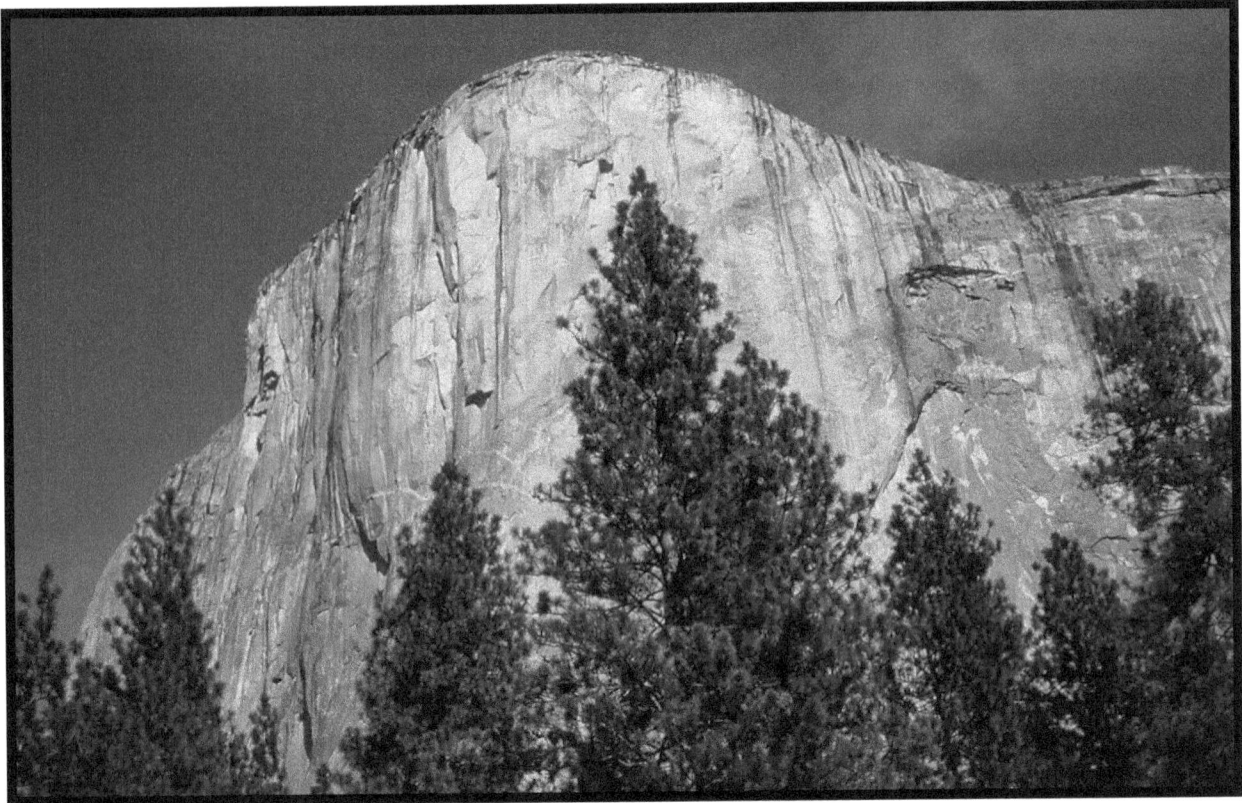

However we begin our spiritual journey – pulled along by the feeling of something missing or caught in a liminal space – over time we come to experience that there is a heart Self, not a part of our ego, that is watching our life and is the key to our spiritual journey. The heart Self has a sense of our life passing by, but it does not seem to grow old. It is the part of the Self that is connected to the Mystery of creation, outside of the ego, which is timeless.

I once heard "patience" described as one of the essential prerequisites of maturity. My immediate thought was that I will never make it. Now it is my perspective that patience is simply a by-product of identifying more deeply with the heart Self that is always in the present moment. The unknowability of the heart Self stems from the fact that we only experience it as a heart perspective on our life. We do not have another internal perspective from which to observe it. Thus, it is always a part of the Mystery of our life that connects us with Mystery outside of ourselves. The realization experience of the heart Self is the first stage of our spiritual journey.

Reflections:

		Further Reflection								
Am I aware of the ineffable Mystery of my heart Self?										

Gratitude

What am I thankful for that will allow me to experience Beauty in my life today?
1.
2.
3.

Awareness of Connection

	Low									High
	1	2	3	4	5	6	7	8	9	10
To Self:										
To Purpose:										
To Mystery/Beauty:										

June 2

The second stage in our spiritual journey is an experience that the heart Self is connected to the heart Mystery of all other humans. For some people that experience is a realization of connection with all sentient beings. Since the heart Self is never experienced as object, it never experiences the Mystery of other heart selves as objects; rather they are experienced as connected to the same Mystery as that in which the heart Self itself participates. Once we put this heart Self into the dogma of a scheme of belief, it will get different names – the transpersonal self, Christ Consciousness, Buddhahood and so on.

In Christian terms, Hell is identification with the limited ego self. Identification with the ego self is the result of sin, or a falling short of not being able to identify with the heart Self, so one is caught in identification with the ego. Heaven, on the other hand, is identification with the Mystery of the heart Self. For Christians that is experienced as living in connection with the Holy Spirit, or living in the Presence of God. Jesus of Nazareth was divine because he, more than anyone else, lived from the heart Self that is the Mystery. We all have this same divine spark, non-ego heart Self, even if it is buried deep under a self-determined ego.

The mystics in all different traditions have developed practices suited for their cultures that allowed them to move into the experience of the heart Self. Their stories recount afterwards the blissful nature of such experiences. But they never are able to describe the experience while in such states, because once the state is made an object of consciousness the connection is lost.

Reflections:

Further Reflection

How might I more deeply experience connection to the Mystery of what is more than me?

Gratitude

What am I thankful for that will allow me to experience Beauty in my life today?
1.
2.
3.

Awareness of Connection

	Low									High
	1	2	3	4	5	6	7	8	9	10

To Self:

To Purpose:

To Mystery/Beauty:

June 3

We move from an ego-centered life to a more heart centered life, when we begin to ask the question: "What does life want me to do?" Or, "What does God want me to do with my life?" Or, "Why am I here?" Or, "If I thought I knew my life's purpose, is it today what I thought it was yesterday?"

Developmentally, we should not skip learning a skill, knowing how to make a living, learning to be responsible for our livelihood in this world. This process of practical learning is somehow a prerequisite to moving beyond the ego's full grasp. But once we have the ego survival skills in place, we all begin to ask larger questions. Sometimes these larger questions seem to be tied to issues of fame, power or money. In that case, the ego is still in charge, just the questions have been super-sized.

But asking the question fiercely, "What is my life for?" is always sure to move us to a deeper level in our spiritual journeys. Just asking the question begins to cut away some of the ego's stubborn scaffolding. Just asking the question begins to move us more deeply into the Mystery of our own lives.

Reflections:

Further Reflection

What does my heart ask of me today?

Gratitude

What am I thankful for that will allow me to experience Beauty in my life today?

1.
2.
3.

Awareness of Connection

	Low 1	2	3	4	5	6	7	8	9	High 10
To Self:										
To Purpose:										
To Mystery/Beauty:										

June 4

The ancient wisdom is that the mental faculty of the mind is not the organ by which we further our spiritual journey. The mind is a wonderful thing, and like many of our human abilities does yeoman service for us in figuring out ways to cope with things in our lives. But it is not the organ by which we gauge our spiritual journey. Just as we don't try to employ the hands to do what the feet do, so we find that we suffer if we try to get the mind to replace the heart as the organ that navigates our spiritual journeys.

Whenever we turn our spiritual journeys over to our minds, we always end up in a crisis of faith. This makes sense. The mind is the organ that, despite all its wonderful characteristics and problem solving abilities, worries. The mind/ego is the part of us that has resentments, that believes all things should work out for the better and has a picture of what that better ought to be.

In the real world we arrive, make connections, do things and die. The mind stumbles at the boundaries of this reality – the beginning and end don't ever really make rational sense. Our spiritual journey is about coming to terms with what does not make logical sense. It is important to understand that the organ to do this with is not the mind but the heart. We spend a lot of time in our lives training the mind. Most of us spend very little time on the task of increasing the capacity for the heart to understand. But nature always moves us in a direction of growth and when we finally come to consider where we are in our own spiritual journeys, we begin the process of growing the capacity of the heart.

Reflections:

Further Reflection

Do I try to manage my spiritual journey with my mind or my heart?

Gratitude

What am I thankful for that will allow me to experience Beauty in my life today?

1.
2.
3.

Awareness of Connection

	Low									High
	1	2	3	4	5	6	7	8	9	10
To Self:										
To Purpose:										
To Mystery/Beauty:										

June 5

Our spiritual journeys start with, and end with, our relationship to Beauty. Let's start at the beginning of this journey. Our childhood spiritual beliefs arise around our experience of the order, harmony, and, if you will, the Beauty of the universe. The mental process of understanding our beliefs is not what gives us our beliefs. Our beliefs are a product of our experience. They involve our whole being as distinct from just our reasoning capacity. So while our beliefs do not produce our spiritual journeys, they do serve as markers along the way of our spiritual experience.

Early religions spent much time and effort and ritual predicting and trying to be in harmony with the seasons of the year. Man looked to the orderliness of nature to provide sufficient game to sustain life and to have adequate rain and sunshine to grow corn, beans and other basic crops. Certain religious rituals emerged around giving thanks for the orderliness of nature that provided the necessary sustenance for life. Another set of religious rituals emerged around trying to implore the gods to restore a natural harmony when it seemed that droughts, floods or other natural events had upset the balance necessary for survival.

Our most basic and primitive spiritual instinct then has to do with our survival, for a yearning for orderliness in life. There is Beauty in the birth of each new dawn, in the return of the season of spring and the abundance of summer.

Our spiritual journeys begin when in some way we recognize and honor the importance of the harmony and Beauty of the natural world.

156

One of the reasons that threats of global warming and ecological disaster penetrate so deeply to our souls is that they threaten the most primal experience of our spirituality.

Reflections:

Further Reflection

How do I recognize and honor the importance of the harmony and Beauty of the natural world?

Gratitude

What am I thankful for that will allow me to experience Beauty in my life today?
1.
2.
3.

Awareness of Connection

	Low									High
	1	2	3	4	5	6	7	8	9	10

To Self:
To Purpose:
To Mystery/Beauty:

June 6

From the orderliness of nature, man developed a sense of inner orderliness, of conscience. We learned morals. We learned the standards of conduct that allowed for an orderly social process. We learned a sense of right and wrong, of rules to protect the weak in society and rules to prevent the abuse of power by the powerful. As a social organism we have incorporated the laws of nature into our social order. Rules of survival have, through much fine tuning, become codes of chivalry and books of etiquette. The Beauty of nature's orderliness has become a way to preserve an orderly society.

Our religious traditions evolved complex rules to help maintain this God given orderliness of nature in our social interactions. As instructive and helpful as these rules may be, their meaning for us lies in our ability to tap the experience of nature's Beauty which is their source.

Reflections:

Further Reflection

Do I appreciate the need for orderliness in my social interactions?

Gratitude

What am I thankful for that will allow me to experience Beauty in my life today?
1.
2.
3.

Awareness of Connection

	Low									High	
	1	2	3	4	5	6	7	8	9	10	

To Self:

To Purpose:

To Mystery/Beauty:

June 7

When the reign of mental discoveries began to shower us in the seventeenth and eighteenth centuries, this age of enlightenment gave birth to the idea of deism. This is the notion that, like the mechanical devices that were then being discovered and put to use, God was the great watchmaker in the sky that set the earth and planets in motion but was otherwise absent from the world. His presence was only the effect of the laws of mechanical theory. Deism is a religion designed by the mind to satisfy the mind's sense of orderliness and harmony. It is a wonderful theory, but it does nothing to satisfy the soul.

Deism is a sophisticated extension of the way primitive religions tried to provide a framework for the orderliness of nature. Most of us at some time are enchanted by the idea of God creating and setting in motion this world governed by exquisitely precise operating laws. But this belief does nothing to help us in time of human need.

Reflections:

How does my need for orderliness of belief serve my spiritual growth?

Gratitude
What am I thankful for that will allow me to experience Beauty in my life today?
1.
2.
3.

Awareness of Connection

	Low									High
	1	2	3	4	5	6	7	8	9	10
To Self:										
To Purpose:										
To Mystery/Beauty:										

June 8

To move beyond the limitations of the mind in our spiritual journeys, we all first become pantheists. Pantheism regards the universe as a manifestation of God. It says there is a spark of God in everything. We don't become pantheist by trying to figure out our beliefs in our heads. We become pantheist because we (and here I mean the big we, all people) regularly experience moments of connection, wonder and Beauty with the world and others.

One of the more vivid of these experiences occurred in 1973 when astronaut Edgar Mitchell was part of the Apollo 14 mission. During the three-day journey back to Earth aboard Apollo 14, Mitchell had an epiphany while looking "down" on the earth from space: "The presence of divinity became almost palpable, and I knew that life in the universe was not just an accident based on random processes…the knowledge came to me directly." Mitchell's experience became famous because he was looking at the earth from space, but such experiences, though perhaps not with the grandeur of Mitchell's, have occurred for all of us in experiencing a sunset or the birth of a child. They are uncommon common experiences that connect us with the divinity that underlies all human experience. With recognition of these experiences, we jump individually, and historically, from a survival experience of God, to a heart experience.

Reflections:

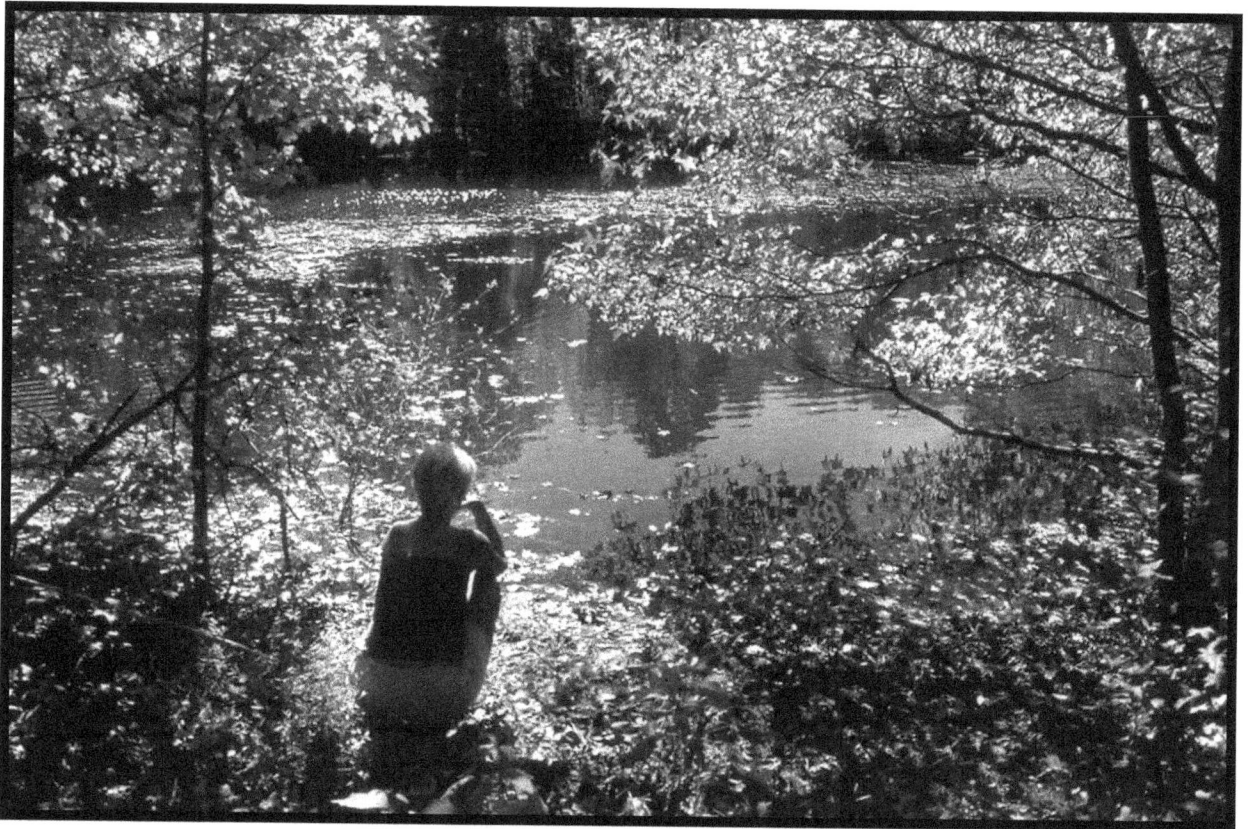

Further Reflection

What does my conscious understanding of God tell me about where I am on my spiritual journey?

Gratitude

What am I thankful for that will allow me to experience Beauty in my life today?

1.
2.
3.

Awareness of Connection

	Low									High
	1	2	3	4	5	6	7	8	9	10
To Self:										
To Purpose:										
To Mystery/Beauty:										

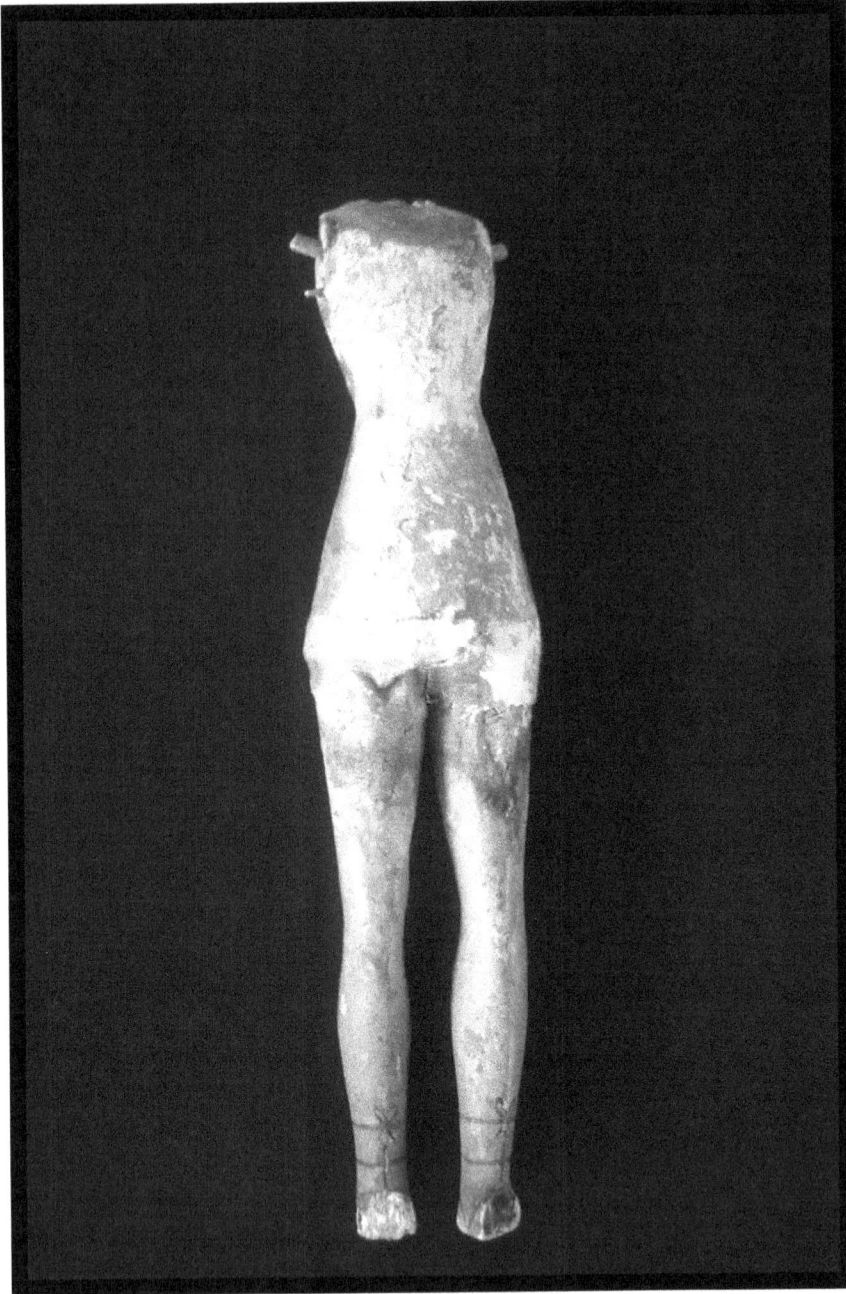

In our movement from a survival experience of God, to a social experience, to a mental experience, to a heart experience, we have stayed in the realm of understanding God as part of orderliness and harmony. This is only half the equation of life – other half is disorganization and chaos. This second half is when we really get into the emotional stew and spiritual journey. We experience a profoundly disorganizing event: a child dies before the parent, we lose a loved one in a totally random accident.

How we come to understand such life-changing, disorganizing events profoundly affects our spiritual journeys. While not in any way discounting the importance of the grief process when it takes time to live through such profoundly disorganizing events, at some point we have to come to terms with the spiritual meaning of this chaos. This is an inner journey. We have moved from the outer world of our spiritual journey with its focus on orderliness to an inner world.

Reflections:

Further Reflection

How have I responded to emotional chaos in my spiritual journey?

Gratitude

What am I thankful for that will allow me to experience Beauty in my life today?

1.
2.
3.

Awareness of Connection

	Low									High
	1	2	3	4	5	6	7	8	9	10

To Self:

To Purpose:

To Mystery/Beauty:

June 10

We first experienced the orderliness of the external world as necessary to our survival, then we experienced the social necessity of orderliness, then we saw that mentally it made sense, then we had an internal, numinous experience of that harmony, a heart experience.

Then we see that the order that so often seems to exist in the external world fails to satisfy our inner world. The Mystery and Beauty of the spiritual meaning of the external world lies in the Beauty of order and symmetry. The Mystery of the spiritual meaning of our inner world comes out of our encounter with our own inner chaos. This inner chaos is always there, but often it is a chaotic external event that triggers the beginning of this internal journey.

Reflections:

Further Reflection
Have I resisted the call of the Mystery of my own internal chaos?

Gratitude
What am I thankful for that will allow me to experience Beauty in my life today?
1.
2.
3.

Awareness of Connection

	Low									High
	1	2	3	4	5	6	7	8	9	10
To Self:										
To Purpose:										
To Mystery/Beauty:										

June 11

Chaos is not easy stuff. On one level we all hate it, and do our utmost to push it away. Yet there is in our soul a part of us that intuitively understands that it is through chaos that we pursue the second half of our spiritual journey.

Uncertainty has a way of leveraging our personal choices. If all were just orderliness, with no unexpected loss and unanticipated grief, then our egos could in actuality pretty much handle our lives. But unexpected loss and unanticipated grief are part of the nature of life. We are born and we bond with people we love and we lose them, sometimes in a seemingly natural progression and at other times for what will always seem the most arbitrary of reasons.

Through the chaos of life, we are initiated into a deeper level of spiritual reality. We can of course refuse this initiation. We can get stuck in "why me?" or some other ego-centered appraisal of the impact of the arbitrariness of life. Or, we can begin to gradually abandon our egos by devotion to spiritual practices that offer us meaning through the chaos.

Reflections:

_____

Further Reflection

Where has the experience of chaos taken me to a deeper level of understanding in my life?

Gratitude

What am I thankful for that will allow me to experience Beauty in my life today?

1.

2.

3.

Awareness of Connection

Low									High
1	2	3	4	5	6	7	8	9	10

To Self:

To Purpose:

To Mystery/Beauty:
_____

June 12

Often our spiritual journeys begin with a serious illness, or some sort of life trauma, that forces us to seek, not rational meaning, but spiritual meaning in uncertainty. This does mean that we have to wait to get bludgeoned by some chaotic event to get to the brass tacks of our spiritual lives. Quite the contrary, those who have undertaken spiritual practices such as prayer and meditation in the more orderly times of their lives, have a real step up when chaos and uncertainty strike. Chaos will come. It always does. Just like orderliness, it is a primary aspect of life. And just as Beauty emerges from our spiritual encounter with harmony, so also does Beauty emerge from our spiritual encounter with chaos.

Reflections:

Further Reflection
Where has chaos taken me deeper into my interior journey of my life? What has it given me?

Gratitude
What am I thankful for that will allow me to experience Beauty in my life today?
1.
2.
3.

Awareness of Connection

	Low									High
	1	2	3	4	5	6	7	8	9	10
To Self:										
To Purpose:										
To Mystery/Beauty:										

June 13

At a time of uncertainty and chaos in our lives, we have choices. We can escape the invitation of chaos by avoidance in the many charming guises of work, indulgences in food, sex or drink, or fantasy. Or, we can allow the encounter with uncertainty to christen our dedication to a greater consciousness.

We wish to be free of the fears of uncertainty – free of the fear of not having a good enough job, of not having enough money, of not finding and/or keeping the right mate. To be free of fear, we have to learn to trust. In fact, a yearning to be able to trust life is an unconscious pull that often gets us started on our spiritual journeys. We want to be able to trust that life is and will be okay.

Both the possibility and the reality of uncertainty and chaos pose spiritual opportunities. We want to be free of the need to control, to be free of the fear of not being good enough, to be free of the need for approval. We in essence want freedom from all the things that the ego thinks it needs to be okay. We want to be enough, to belong, to be accepted by something greater than ourselves.

We want connection with what is greater than ourselves. We want our own wholeness and connection with what we intuit is a divine force that holds that wholeness.

As our spiritual journey deepens, we may realize that we want to connect with a loving and caring God.

Reflections:

Further Reflection

Am I willing to answer the questions that my uncertainty asks of me?

Gratitude

What am I thankful for that will allow me to experience Beauty in my life today?

1.
2.
3.

Awareness of Connection

	Low									High
	1	2	3	4	5	6	7	8	9	10
To Self:										
To Purpose:										
To Mystery/Beauty:										

June 14

Once we commit ourselves to the possibility of greater connection to consciousness and meaning in the world, we invite in all the possibilities that chaos offers.

Chaos theory is defined as the branch of mathematics that deals with complex systems whose behavior is highly sensitive to slight changes in conditions, so that small alterations can give rise to strikingly great consequences. In theological terms through the alignment of our conscious intentions with a meaning greater than ourselves, we open ourselves up to the possibility of Grace. Grace is the Beauty that comes from chaos.

At this stage of our spiritual journeys, our lives may seem outwardly as ordinary as ever, but the interior journey has begun in earnest. A sure sign is experiencing a calling, that we are called to do something special in this world (something special in the sense that somehow we are especially suited to do it). This something special may be quite ordinary, but will offer us a way to have a greater experience of the Beauty of our creative interaction with others and the Divine.

Reflections:

| Further Reflection |
| How open am I today to possibilities of chaos in my life? |

Further Reflection

How open am I today to possibilities of chaos in my life?

Gratitude

What am I thankful for that will allow me to experience Beauty in my life today?

1.

2.

3.

Awareness of Connection

	Low									High
	1	2	3	4	5	6	7	8	9	10
To Self:										
To Purpose:										
To Mystery/Beauty:										

June 15

To be good at sports, an athlete has to train. To progress in one's spiritual journey, the discipline of training is also necessary. Like athletic training, spiritual training is developmental. The most helpful training depends upon where we are along the road. The formula of the twelve steps of Alcoholics Anonymous gives a good recipe for the first stages.

In the first stage, we come to believe at an emotional level that we don't have all the answers and that there is help outside of ourselves in finding greater wisdom for our lives. Next, we do a thorough job of becoming aware of all the patterns in our life that limit our connection to self, God and others. These patterns are largely based upon fears – fear of material insecurity, emotional insecurity and social/sexual insecurity.

Once we understand the patterns by which we try to protect ourselves from our fears and insecurities, we become willing to let go of these patterns. Then we review our life, and wherever we have caused harm, we go back (as long as it will not create more harm) and make amends – that is, we set things right. We engage in restorative justice.

Only after all this has been done are we ready for the next level of spiritual training. This next level focuses on prayer and meditation.

The Twelve Steps of Alcoholics Anonymous make clear that listening silently for God will not be that productive if we have not first sought to remove our emotional defenses that block us from ourselves and God, clearing our psychic attics and basements of old resentments and guilts. It is hard to wait silently on God when our emotions keep coming back to feelings of guilt and shame.

176

In other words, before the radio transmitter of the soul can be tuned into God, we have to get rid of all the static and interference caused by the defenses we created to help us survive, and right the wrongs that we have done because of those emotional defenses. Once the interference is cleared up, then the possibility of communication with something greater than self begins in the silence of our hearts.

Reflections:

<u>Further Reflection</u>
Have I done the initial stage work of clearing my mind and emotions so I can be available to dialogue with God?

<u>Gratitude</u>
What am I thankful for that will allow me to experience Beauty in my life today?
1.
2.
3.

<u>Awareness of Connection</u>

	Low									High
	1	2	3	4	5	6	7	8	9	10
To Self:										
To Purpose:										
To Mystery/Beauty:										

June 16

Once the basic work of clearing old patterns has been done, what is the training regime like for the next phase of our spiritual growth?

The bad news is that a focus on mental prayer, listening to tapes of your favorite mentor and an occasional massage is not going to be sufficient. The good news is that by now, once we are in a cleared state, our longing for an experience of God is deeper, feels more fundamentally a part of who we are. It is a dual longing that may be experienced simply as a sense of yearning. The two aspects of this longing are the pull toward knowing God and the pull toward knowing the spark of divinity within ourselves.

We begin to sense that finding our own greatest potential is tied up with experiencing emotional freedom. To arrive at a place of emotional freedom, we must experience the world as safe, that all is truly okay. To feel free we must have an emotional reality that sees all the suffering in the world, and still believes deeply in the goodness of our lives. We no longer fear being ourselves and we no longer fear God. The aspects of our spiritual life that we must strengthen to be in the place of liberation, or nirvana or Heaven on Earth, are our faith and our courage.

We build faith by daily seeking to increase our trust. Trust is built by practices of thankfulness. We build courage by daily taking small risks that move us closer to ourselves, to God and to others.

Reflections:

Further Reflection

What risks am I willing to take today to move closer to self, God and others?

Gratitude

What am I thankful for that will allow me to experience Beauty in my life today?
1.
2.
3.

Awareness of Connection

	Low									High
	1	2	3	4	5	6	7	8	9	10
To Self:										
To Purpose:										
To Mystery/Beauty:										

June 17

On our spiritual journeys, we would all love to have a Moses burning bush experience. Many of us have prayed, particularly in a time of need or uncertainty: "God tell me what to do?" "What is my truth?" Foxhole prayer is not usually the way that we are led to connect with a wisdom greater than ourselves.

Some of us are born and grow up with an easy access to an intuitive sense of knowing. It is heart knowledge. Or gut knowledge. Over time, we learn that it is sometimes not right, and that we may need to get a second opinion, but we learn that we can rely on our deeper inner intuitive sense of knowing most of the time.

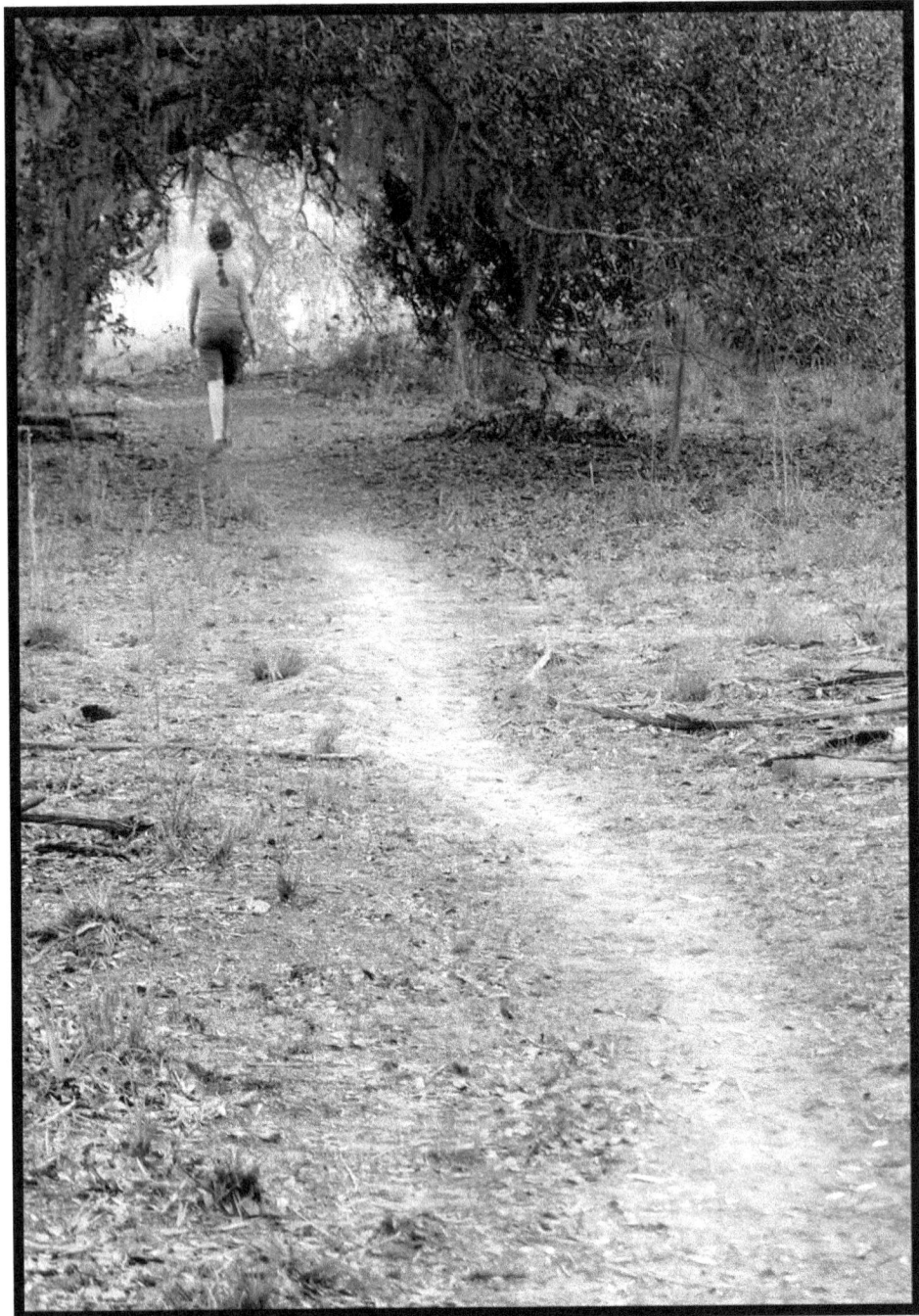

Others of us, sometimes in childhood, were made to feel that this intuitive sense of knowing was not right, or could not be believed. As adults we don't have easy access to this place of connection to our own wisdom, or if we do, we don't trust it.

We may have a certain pervasive anxiety that keeps us from being able to fully access our own wisdom. Many of us with this kind of childhood wounding have a special gift for the nuances of truth, but must give some dedicated time to learning to trust our gut and heart wisdom.

If intuitive knowing is weak, we just start practicing. In ordinary decisions, rather than making a mental habit decision, we take a moment to focus on our heart, or gut, to see what sense of a decision comes from that place. Following the arc of decisions made from a more intuitive place –

what sort of outcomes are there? How do these outcomes compare with decisions just made out of mental habit?

Reflections:

Further Reflection

Am I able to connect with my inner sense of knowing? Am I willing to strengthen the muscle of this knowing?

Gratitude

What am I thankful for that will allow me to experience Beauty in my life today?
1.
2.
3.

Awareness of Connection

	Low									High
	1	2	3	4	5	6	7	8	9	10
To Self:										
To Purpose:										
To Mystery/Beauty:										

June 18

A friend once told me that he had never seen a burning bush, but he had learned to pay attention to many smoldering ones. By strengthening our sense of intuitive knowing, we may not be able to feel we are directly spoken to by God, but we are much more likely to experience a smoldering bush. Though we long to hear a message aloud from God, the lack of audible (either interiorly or exteriorly) messages does not foreclose the possibility of dialogue with what is greater than ourselves.

The Christian term Holy Spirit is often referred to as the Spirit of Truth. When our intuitive knowing gives us the sense of the truth about something, we are having a dialogue with something greater than ourselves. We may do a mental analysis and decide – yes, this is the course of action we should take. Then we sit with it, perhaps pray about it, and if we get back a sense of intuitive knowing that this is our truth, we have in fact been in a dialogue with something greater than ourselves. Or, we may have an idea of what we should do and we talk it over with a trustworthy friend. After our conversation with our friend, we are in a different perspective about the choices we face. We may see more possibilities and better options. Somehow something outside ourselves has given us a more truth filled perspective.

Occasionally such expanded knowing will point toward a smoldering bush. We will become aware that there is some opportunity, or idea, in our lives that is pulling us. It may not be God speaking to us directly, but we have a choice: we can neglect the smoldering or we can stay attentive to it. We can blow on the coals. We can see what opportunity may be offered to us that we have hardly been aware of.

Reflections:

How can I engage in dialogue with a greater wisdom than myself?

Gratitude
What am I thankful for that will allow me to experience Beauty in my life today?
1.
2.
3.

Awareness of Connection

	Low									High
	1	2	3	4	5	6	7	8	9	10
To Self:										
To Purpose:										
To Mystery/Beauty:										

June 19

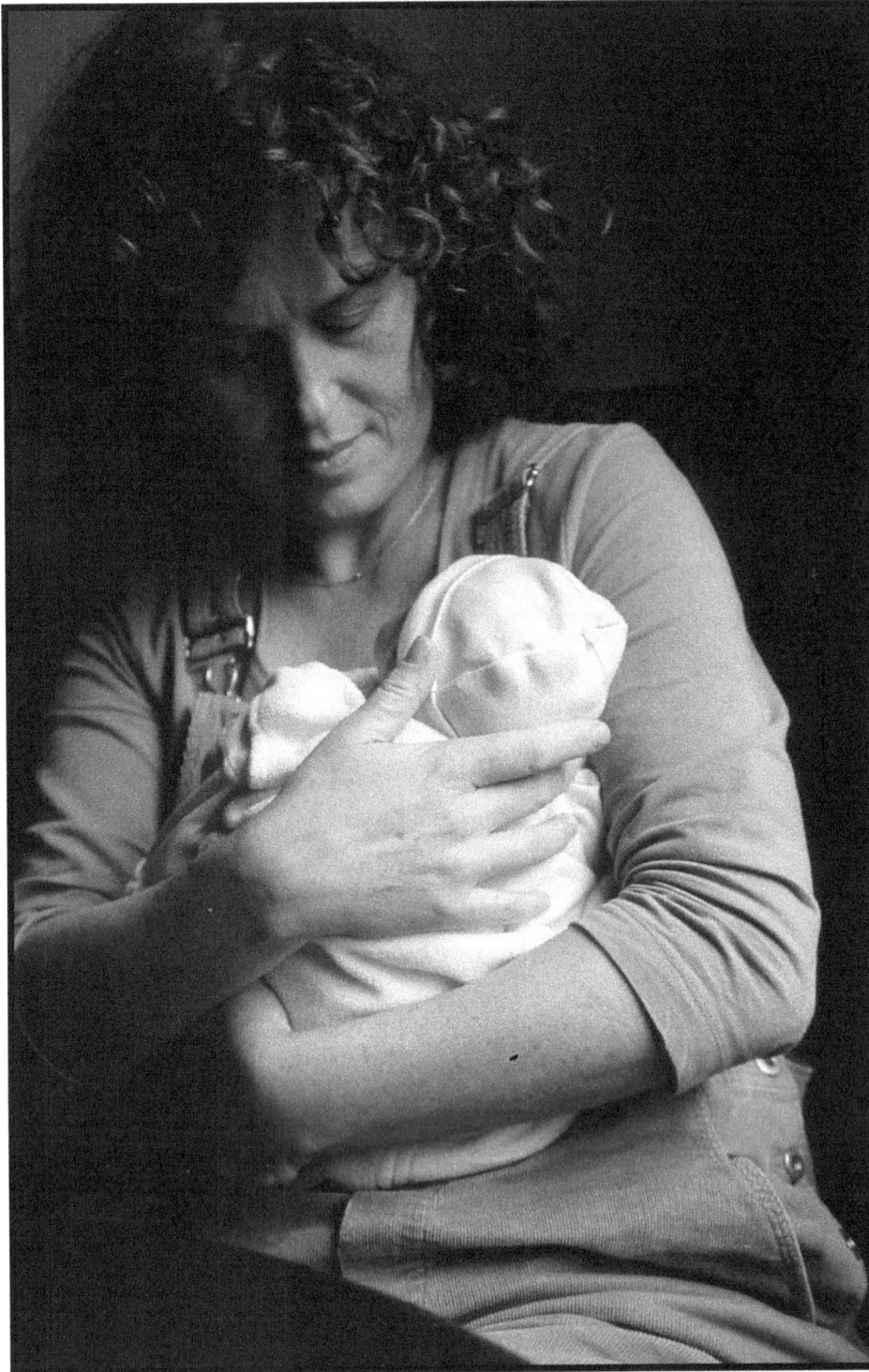

Once we learn to be on the lookout for smoldering bushes, then we have the opportunity to develop different ways to communicate with what has not yet fully sprung to life in our lives. If our psychic house is cleared we can spend time in prayer and meditation – prayer, not of mental habit, but of our body, emotions and heart. This prayer brings all of us to the dialogue.

Often it is necessary to make one creative step forward with an open mind to receive back from the world a creative answer. Our actions become a form of dialogue with God.

Here is the formula. We take an action toward where our intuitive knowing pulls us. After the action we are aware of what is experienced. Is there a sense of rightness, of bringing more of our life to bear in the world? Or do we experience anger or upset?

Our actions, and our experience of those actions, is a form of dialogue that includes what is greater than ourselves. We see this when we experience an action, our reaction to that action and then have a knowing that is greater than the two. We experience that something of Beauty is created.

<u>Reflections</u>:

<u>Further Reflection</u>
How can I listen to the dialogue with God that comes from paying attention to my actions?

<u>Gratitude</u>
What am I thankful for that will allow me to experience Beauty in my life today?
1.
2.
3.

<u>Awareness of Connection</u>

	Low									High
	1	2	3	4	5	6	7	8	9	10
To Self:										
To Purpose:										
To Mystery/Beauty:										

June 20

We now see how the old religious argument of faith versus works is misplaced. Our actions, what we do, are simply a part of a dialogue with what we believe. The deeper we get into that dialogue the more opportunity there is for Beauty, for Grace. Grace doesn't depend solely upon either. Rather discernment of Grace depends upon the dialogue. The dialogue is the opportunity for something new to enter our thoughts, feelings and lives. When it does we have an experience we call Grace.

Reflections:

Further Reflection
Am I in a monologue? How can I be in a dialogue?

Gratitude
What am I thankful for that will allow me to experience Beauty in my life today?
1.
2.
3.

Awareness of Connection

	Low									High
	1	2	3	4	5	6	7	8	9	10
To Self:										
To Purpose:										
To Mystery/Beauty:										

Appendix

Daily Examine/Inventory

Part One

Indicate a percentage for the time during the day the trait or quality was present –

I was:

1. Fully present

2. Connected to and holding center

3. Meeting fear directly from center

4. Listening at a deep level

5. Making decisions by listening fully to heart, head and instinctual center

6. Forgiving those who have harmed me

7. Choosing not to feel rejected but a part of

8. Reaching out and taking action to be a part of and to belong

9. Taking action to show my emotional truth

188

10. Staying with and not running from an uncomfortable emotion

11. Was I 100% into my own life

12. Was I able to stay with longing without needing to escape it in an attempt to satisfy it

13. Was I connected to something greater than self

14. Was I able to do something special today to celebrate being alive

Daily Examine/Inventory

Part Two

When in distress practice awareness, acceptance and action

<u>Awareness</u>

1. The situation causing me discomfort is

_____

2. I am upset with _____ (person, principle, institution) because

_____

3. Because of what happened I feel

_____

<u>Acceptance</u>

1. I lovingly recognize and accept without judgment my feelings.

Willing_____ Open_____ Skeptical _____ Unwilling_____

2. I accept my feelings as a reflection of my beliefs about how I see this situation.

Willing_____ Open_____ Skeptical _____ Unwilling_____

3. Even though I may not like to feel as I do, I accept that by allowing my feelings about this situation to be, I may learn and grow.

Willing_____ Open_____ Skeptical _____ Unwilling_____

4. My distress is a signal that I am a) resentful _____ b) selfish_____ c) dishonest_____ d) afraid_____ or e) _____.

5. I notice that these feelings repeat a pattern in my life and that I have had similar experiences where I was unable to accept fully my feelings and let go of them. For example_____

6. I realize that the distress I feel now may be part of a pattern when some situation stirs in me feelings that I have disowned, denied, repressed and projected onto another.

Willing_____ Open_____ Skeptical _____ Unwilling_____

7. This situation is reflecting_____ which I need to love and accept about myself.

8. I release the need to blame and to be right, and I am willing to see the situation causing my discomfort as the lesson I need right now.

Willing_____ Open_____ Skeptical _____ Unwilling_____

9. I realize that trapped within my own ego I will not be able to change this pattern or my feeling reaction.

Willing_____ Open_____ Skeptical _____ Unwilling_____

10. I realize that by taking action to connect to Beauty and what is important to me beyond self, that this situation may lead to healing for me and others.

Willing_____ Open_____ Skeptical _____ Unwilling_____

Action

1. I give thanks to life and to _____ (whatever caused the discomfort) for giving me this opportunity to experience my feelings more deeply and for mirroring my projections.

Willing_____ Open_____ Skeptical _____ Unwilling_____

2. I turn all my feeling of distress over to what is beyond me.

Willing_____ Open_____ Skeptical _____ Unwilling_____

3. I will pray for _____ (person, principle or institution) causing this opportunity for my healing and for their well-being and peace.

Willing_____ Open_____ Skeptical _____ Unwilling_____

4. I realize that through my resentment, selfishness, dishonesty, or fear I was experiencing the situation as a victim and that I can re-frame the situation as follows:

_____

5. If I am still feeling stuck in distress, I am willing to pick up the phone and call someone who is trustworthy to share aloud this worksheet and my feelings.

`Willing_____ Open_____ Skeptical _____ Unwilling_____

6. I completely forgive myself for my feelings and surrender them. If I have caused any harm I am willing to make amends, and I ask God's forgiveness and for acceptance of myself as a loving, generous and creative person.

Willing_____ Open_____ Skeptical _____ Unwilling_____

7. I pray that I may use this experience to more fully be of service to my fellow man and I will look for the opportunity to do so.

Willing_____ Open_____ Skeptical _____ Unwilling_____

www.ingramcontent.com/pod-product-compliance
Lightning Source LLC
Chambersburg PA
CBHW081254040426

42452CB00014B/2496